"*Witnessing and Psychoanalysis* explores the silent zones of the foundation of being. With the support of writers like Melville, Hölderlin, Kafka and Celan, this investigation takes the reader to the boundaries of the gap created in the psyche by trauma. Réfabert goes beyond the Winnicottian 'mirror'; he helps us to rethink the negative from the perspective of a parental psychic matrix. The author shows how the blunted zones of this matrix and the gaps created by trauma are compensated by the construction of a fetish or a scenario used as a substitute mirror serving to reflect a man or a woman wandering the earth without a shadow. This collection of essays is an extraordinary source of inspiration for clinicians, psychoanalysts, theoreticians and literary critics."

Carlo Bonomi

"Philippe Réfabert's book *Witnessing and Psychoanalysis* takes the reader on a journey beyond the usual references of mainstream psychoanalysis and proposes concepts such as 'soul murder', 'paradoxical foundation' and 'trace of death' as tools for the analyst in his work. 'Soul murder' also characterises patients who experienced extreme trauma, and who challenge the analyst to work with muted portions of his psyche of which he is unaware. Starting from the author's efforts to free himself from institutional constraints and become an analyst for such patients, the book offers a wealth of clinical examples, showing, for example, how a child can be expected to animate a mortally wounded mother, a situation left unacknowledged for lack of a witness. Réfabert's proposed paradigm for psychoanalysis in such cases is enlightened by Pirandello's *Six Characters in Search of an Author*, which summons the analyst to climb on the stage in order to be present on the side of the patient to witness and create authorship for matters which have been thrown into nonexistence. I strongly recommend the reading of this book, which constitutes a landmark for psychoanalysis in our era of catastrophic events with their resulting traumas."

Françoise Davoine

Witnessing and Psychoanalysis

Psychoanalysis and Witnessing intertwines aspects of the history of psychoanalysis with the development of Philippe Réfabert's own thinking and clinical practice.

Réfabert's work invites analysts to reflect on the inception of psychic life. The author argues for a revision of drive theory and reflects on the psychic functioning of the analyst in the session. Réfabert forces the analyst to see the necessity of standing witness to acts left unacknowledged; he holds that in analysis witnessing is crucial.

With case material from the author's practice throughout, this book will be of great interest to psychoanalysts in practice and in training.

Philippe Réfabert is a psychoanalyst and prolific author based in Paris, France. His previous book, *From Freud to Kafka*, is also published by Routledge.

Witnessing and Psychoanalysis

As If It Never Happened

Philippe Réfabert
Translated by Agnès Jacob

Routledge
Taylor & Francis Group

LONDON AND NEW YORK

First published in English 2024 by Routledge
by Routledge
4 Park Square, Milton Park, Abingdon, Oxon OX14 4RN

and by Routledge
605 Third Avenue, New York, NY 10158

Routledge is an imprint of the Taylor & Francis Group, an informa business

© 2024 Éditions Campagne Première

Translated by Agnès Jacob

The right of Philippe Réfabert to be identified as author of this work has been asserted in accordance with sections 77 and 78 of the Copyright, Designs and Patents Act 1988.

Published in French by Éditions Campagne Première, 2018

British Library Cataloguing-in-Publication Data
A catalogue record for this book is available from the British Library

Library of Congress Cataloging-in-Publication Data
Names: Réfabert, Philippe, author. | Jacob, Agnès, translator.
Title: Witnessing and psychoanalysis : as if it never happened /
Philippe Réfabert ; translated by Agnès Jacob.
Other titles: Comme si de rien. English Description: Abingdon,
Oxon ; New York, NY : Routledge, 2024. | "Published in French by
Éditions Campagne Première, 2018"—Title page verso. | Includes
bibliographical references and index. |
Identifiers: LCCN 2023019061 (print) | LCCN 2023019062
(ebook) | ISBN 9781032564760 (hardback) | ISBN 9781032564746
(paperback) | ISBN 9781003435730 (ebook)
Subjects: LCSH: Psychoanalysis.
Classification: LCC BF173 .R368513 2024 (print) | LCC BF173
(ebook) | DDC 150.19/5—dc23/eng/20230523
LC record available at https://lccn.loc.gov/2023019061
LC ebook record available at https://lccn.loc.gov/2023019062

ISBN: 978-1-032-56476-0 (hbk)
ISBN: 978-1-032-56474-6 (pbk)
ISBN: 978-1-003-43573-0 (ebk)

DOI: 10.4324/9781003435730

Typeset in Times New Roman
by codeMantra

Contents

Foreword

Slow progress in analysis

I ventured into the field of psychoanalysis with great trepidation. I had been directed to start a therapeutic analysis with one of the members of the Paris Psychoanalytic Society (SPP). Later, a commission would decide whether or not this would be considered a teaching analysis, provided it had been conducted by one of the full members of the Society, the only accredited teaching analysts. Pierre Mâle, one of the members of this commission, suggested that I see Christian David, an analyst who had recently become a full member. This was at the start of the 1960s.

I went to see him. My first dream: as a small child, I saw myself stuck between two buses. The interpretation was that the two buses were my parents. The analysis was on its way.

At the time I was an intern in psychiatry in the *Hôpitaux de la Seine* network, and was entrusted with providing therapy to patients. Jean Oury, a psychiatrist at the La Borde clinic whom I had met while attending Lacan's seminars, advised me to discuss a very difficult patient with Gisela Pankow. She diagnosed hysterical psychosis and admitted me to the group under her supervision. In these group sessions, madness came alive. My interest in these sessions contrasted greatly with the drowsiness that overcame me on my analyst's couch. Pankow's sessions were an exquisite foundational experience for me. She did not belong to any recognised psychoanalytic society and her teaching was not part of any formal system. When I left these sessions with Gisela Pankow, I sometimes had to park my Citroën on the side of the road to give free reign to my urge to laugh and laugh. I had found my place; a part of my being was in sympathy with the prominent place granted here to the traumatic in the genesis of madness.

At first I thought that the burst of laughter revealed the sharp conflict between the child in me, the one to whom Pankow spoke, and the person who wanted to be admitted to the SPP and strove, with the complicity of his analyst, to confirm drive theory as best he could, along with the accepted doctrine in which the sexual, taken literally, usurps the place of the traumatic. Despite wanting to be admitted to the Society, this good disciple contested as best he could the Oedipus complex as formulated in 1900... by sleeping on the couch. I kept having the feeling that the training dispensed by this institution was insufficient. I was determined—without making a conscious decision—to seek on the margins what I was not finding at the centre: "Getting inside the outside", as André de Bouchet phrased it, according to Henri Maldiney.

And so, far from the mother institution, with Pankaw, I was filled with wonder, a wonder that contrasted with the sadness and anxiety I felt when listening to lectures given by some members of the SPP. I remember especially a talk given by Serge Lebovici on Winnicott's work. Lebovici was laying the groundwork for the official condemnation that would cast a shadow on the work of this analyst, whose practice was presented as a mothering deviation of psychoanalysis. Winnicott was said to have eliminated the "father"—seen as the representative of the law—and consequently castration, the "symbolic" debt that according to the doctrine is indissociably tied to the figure of the father. This description of Winnicott's work is still circulating today. Recently, 50 years later, on the occasion of a conference where I was invited by François Lévy to discuss his lecture on Bion, I found a way to tell Serge Lebovici, and teachers of psychoanalysis, that the principle of the Oedipus complex—its principle, not its psychological reduction—was very firmly held and defended by Winnicott. I will come back to this.

I remember another lecture, this one given by Béla Grunberger. This highly respected analyst was explaining how we should look at Ferenczi and his work. He presented Ferenczi as a brilliant child whose work was admirable as long as its author submitted to the "paternal law", that is, to the letter of Freud's doctrine. I was told that evening that Ferenczi had strayed from this "law of the father", to end up in a maternal deviation that drove him mad, according to Ernest Jones, a false witness. In Jones' biography of Freud, considered at the time the definitive reference, we can still read how this disciple falsifies confidences and deforms the end of a life to bring down on his detested former analyst a diagnosis of paranoia. (Jones had undergone a short analysis with Ferenczi, to whom Freud had referred him. He remained frustrated that he was not analysed by the master, but above all, he was aware that Ferenczi did not think highly of his moral qualities. On this subject, I refer the reader to the text on Jones by Barbro Sylwan, in the book we co-authored.[1]) This diagnosis of paranoia was the first of a series inflicted on certain analysts: after Ferenczi, it was Nicolas Abraham. Why were they afflicted with this label? No doubt because both of them took into account the larger context, the traumatic circumstance contributing to produce psycho-corporal suffering. This diagnosis was inflicted on analysts who freed themselves from Freud's hypnotic hold and opened new paths. I must admit that I myself inflicted this diagnosis on this or that analysand who caused me difficulties, until I was able to turn myself around and recognise a blunder, a mistake, a resistance, and take into account the part I played in the persecutory crisis the patient was going through.

After Ferenczi, it was Nicolas Abraham's turn to be subjected to such persecution. Béla Grunberger, one of the most sought-after teaching analysts, had been his analyst, as well as that of his partner, Maria Torok. He had also been the analyst of Barbro Sylwan, who was a friend of the couple, as well as a friend of Janine

Chasseguet-Smirgel, Grunberger's partner. Imbroglio. Saying this today reveals the degree to which Oedipal and drive psychology had priority over a clear understanding of the psychic space of an individual. It also shows how much—before Ferenczi made theory and practice congruent—it influenced individuals as knowledgeable and mindful of the truth as the future would reveal them to be.

To go back to Béla Grunberger's lecture on Ferenczi and his work, I remember that what I felt on such occasions resembled what I felt when attending clinical presentations where Freudian constructs were very similar to the ready-made methods I encountered in my analysis. The fits of laughter that caused me to stop my car when I left the sessions with Pankow were related to my being pulled in two different directions—not because they revealed the conflict that split me into two parts, cancelling each other out, as I first thought—but because this was an unexpected tear in the curtain of conformity. The euphoria I felt after the group supervision sessions with Pankow sprang from the discovery of a colourful and vibrant landscape into which it was possible to venture. Although it was still unknown to me, it held out promise.

All things considered, I never forgot this initial wonderment and my admiration for Pankow's work. She was the first relay station in the analytic world, but outside the Society where I was receiving my training, where what was said resonated with the world (that of my childhood), my world and that of poets, novelists and artists. My supervision with Pankow ended abruptly when the patient made a suicide attempt during a session. Looking back, I can see that when I started out I was repeatedly falling into a trap that took me several decades to understand before I freed myself from it. My analyst, Christian David, together with Gisela Pankow and this patient, as well as Grunberger, made up the cast of characters I brought together in Polonius' hideout, on the stage of my theatre. And they were willing to play their parts. The patient by scarifying her arms during the sessions, Pankow who did not stop this crazy game—did not call my analyst into question, as she often did for the other members of the group, who were all in analysis with Lacan: "But what is your analyst doing, exactly?" she would ask in an exasperated tone. As for Christian David, he did not think of asking himself, and asking me—his analysand—what was being repeated. What was even more serious was that he did not consider the question so as to suggest it to me at the right moment. What was I repeating? It was the attitude of an all-powerful mother, the actual mothering excess of someone who could not say "enough" to her *furor sanendi* and place limits where they should be. Later, I learned that one of Christian David's analysands had thrown herself out of a window; that Gisela Pankow, my supervisor, had applied for membership in the International Psychoanalytical Association; and that she was a close friend of Béla Grunberger, whose support she counted on to be admitted to the IPA. Later still, I understood the potential perverse effects of belonging to any analytical association. These associations are needed, of course, but the network of friendships and common interests they create must recede, fall away, disappear altogether in the analyst's office.

At the end of the 1960s I was reading Freud's work diligently. I was reading it in translation with my colleagues, but I didn't find much pleasure in this, and the texts did not resonate with me. At the same time, I was pursuing my training in my own way and for the most part outside the SPP, with Jean Laplanche, who conducted a seminar at the École normale supérieure, in the Cavaillès lecture hall, named after a famous *resistant*. I appreciated Laplanche's patient reading of Freud's texts, which elucidated them, placing them in perspective and showing the underlying thinking process. I acquired useful work tools, while my analysis went on uneventfully.

Laplanche's article "Fantasy and the Origins of Sexuality", co-authored with Pontalis and published in 1964 in *Les Temps Modernes*, [2] had great importance for me. The point that caught my attention and continued to support my thinking was that after Freud abandoned the theory of seduction in 1897, his unsuccessful but relentless search for evidence of a sexual–presexual event in the history of each patient—not only at the start of his practice, but until the very end—reinforced the idea of sexual constitution—after making a detour through phylogenesis, to arrive at last at originary fantasies, all of them testifying to the "already there". This persistent research lived on after Freud's death in some of his disciples, like Kurt Fissler, who kept trying to extract the primal scene from Sergei Pankejeff, the Wolf Man. Leaving behind seduction theory reinforced the innate and thereby amputated psychoanalytic thought of the "traumatic", giving itself, through the notion of constitution, an appendage resembling a wooden leg. It was not until 1949, when "Confusion of the Tongues" was published in English, that we discovered that Ferenczi had alerted Freud and the other analysts as early as 1932 to the need for a revision of the theory:

> Insufficiently deep exploration of the exogenous factor leads to the danger of resorting prematurely to explanations in terms of 'disposition' and 'constitution'.[3]

Based on what I had already worked out, as well as on what I didn't know that I knew, I published in the journal *Revue française de psychoanalyse* an article entitled "Disavowal, repudiation".[4] The article was a critique of Freud's 1927 text "Fetishism"; in it, I argued that in order for a representation to be inscribed, it had to be the case that the marble plaque, the support of the inscription, be there, having withstood the violence of trauma rather than being destroyed by it. Without knowing it, I had just laid out the premises of the work that would be my focus for years to come: soul murder. It was the only written contribution I ever made to the SPP.

My second contribution—oral this time—was made in a training seminar. It was a text analysis of *Beyond the Pleasure Principle*. This analysis, on which I worked in an almost trance-like state, was my first true encounter with Freud—with his genius. I was fascinated with the leap made by this man who, at the age of 63, would leave some impatient disciples and some less than rigorous minds speechless. My research, which I never published, has nourished all my subsequent work. It is the foundations which allows me to call myself a Freudian. Looking back, it was the first time that I encountered the figure of the paradox clearly spelled out, and the extraordinary idea of a single drive, an advance that Freud immediately discarded for reasons of "common sense"—but to what extent could this apply to a daring mind such as his?

In May 1968 I was working as a therapist at the Alfred Binet medical centre. Some of my colleagues and I started a "revolution": we wanted to reorganise the work structure, to eliminate certain separations, especially between doctors and psychologists. The director, Serge Lebovici, somewhat frazzled during this merry month of May, asked me to come and talk to him about the changes we were introducing in the institution. He told me that all this upheaval required too many meetings and made him too tired. To conclude, he gave me his interpretation: I was trying to kill the father. This arbitrary generalisation based on a simplified psychological reading of the Oedipus complex sent chills down my spine.

I found my way out of the trap as blindly as I had walked into it. I spoke at a public clinical meeting of the SPP—with Grunberger-Polonius present—to discuss the account made in analysis by a man who repeated in nocturnal tribulations the traumas inflicted by bad treatment and murderous attacks in his childhood in Corsica by mean grandmothers, witches and spell casters. A few weeks later I asked to be admitted to the Society as an affiliated member. My request was denied and, to my own surprise, I was not surprised. One of the "much needed ones", as Lacan so eloquently called associate members—while referring to affiliated members as "on their toes"—conveyed the decision to me. He said he was sorry, but a certain analyst had informed the commission that my membership was not desirable. While we talked, I was able to learn from this messenger that the prohibition came from Grunberger, who had "not liked what I said."

In 1969, Grunberger and his companion co-authored a book using a joint pseudonym—André Stéphane—giving it the outrageous title *Universe of Protest*. The authors claimed to be making a psychoanalytic reading of the May 1968 student revolts. In truth, the analysis was limited to psychologising drive theory and the Oedipus complex, laid out in the book with self-satisfied arrogance. If I would have trusted what I felt during Grunberger's lecture on Ferenczi, I would have seen sooner what form totalising thinking was taking in the psychoanalytic universe. Later, thanks to René Major, I learned what Béla Grunberger was capable of—and the psychoanalytic institution along with him. In the early 1970s, Nicolas Abraham, whose work was substantial by then, worried about having been refused as an associate member of the SPP for the umpteenth time. After much reflection, and after talking about his friends and colleagues who were full members, he concluded that what stood in the way could only come from his analyst. When his friend René Major was named director of the training institute of the SPP, Abraham asked him to look in the archives for a possible trace of Grunberger's intervention. Indeed, René Major found two letters in which Grunberger was issuing a warning against his analysand to the commission. Major wrote a coded text, "The clandestine letter", in which he related these events. Maria Torok exposed this appalling incident in greater detail in the journal *Le Coq-Héron*, in an issue dedicated to Abraham's work and her own.[5]

In fact, the visceral reactions I had to these totalitarian manifestations were familiar to me: I had experienced them in my childhood, when one of my parents blamed me for something he had unknowingly provoked in me. I define "totalitarian thinking" as that of someone who is unable to turn back on himself. He causes the child to go mad, by remaining deaf to the messages the child sends him in the language at his disposal: gestures, facial expressions… perhaps before having to resort to refusing to eat. The language I invented during my first analysis consisted of nodding off.

I resigned from this Society in 1973. It was crucial for me to come back armed with the knowledge set aside when trauma theory was abandoned. Was it not the case that unknown crimes, betrayals, and secrets big and small prepared the ground for early seduction, leading to disguised abandonments or silent complicities at the root of acts akin to incest? In this context, I later proposed the notion of a psychic matrix made up of the totality of virtual inscriptions, where every event has its place, except one traumatic event whose absence creates a vast gap.

The infant placed in such a matrix will stubbornly position himself before this gap to demand an answer in the place where the parent sends no echo, or acts as if the child is harassing him. When the parent has suffered soul murder, the child is immobilised, held to the injunction of responding and not responding to the call coming from the living child in the parent, a hurt and impossible-to-abandon child whose plea is inevitable. The infant's answer runs up against the relentless character of the guardian in the parent. In analysis, transference reproduces this contradiction. In *The Interpretation of Dreams*, Freud says: "the child with all his impulses survives"; as an analyst, this is what I must take into account.

At the time, this return to trauma theory reinforced the validity of the figures Gisela Pankow brought to life—those inhabiting the circles of hell: the impatient, the lazy, the faint-hearted, the traitors, the cowardly, the thieves, the informers, the counterfeiters, the murderers, the false witnesses, the envious, the slanderers, the rascals and scoundrels and, last but not least, the living dead. Pankow strove to bring these figures to light, to give them faces and names that their families had denied them or had concealed. The human comedy awakened like Sleeping Beauty, and psychoanalysis with her, recovering its vitality and rising to the level of Shakespeare, Cervantes, Montaigne, Goethe, Mozart and Da Ponte among others, with whom Freud was well acquainted.

This is what Pankow's teaching had revealed to me. Now, I was feeling alone and discouraged. But just then, I met Barbro Sylwan. She listened to the obstinate man I was then, continuing on with my analyst and, as my friends often said, finding ways to saw off the branch I was sitting on. Sylwan had written a text about the analysis of little Hans, recounting an episode in the life of this five-year-old boy. Her text depicted Freud running up the stairs leading to the Graf's apartment two at a time, with a gift under his arm. It was a rocking hose for Herbert, the little boy who came to be known as Hans—the son of Olga Hönig-Gref, Freud's analysand. Barbro Sylwan and I decided to work together based on our shared conviction that the fervor which had brought psychoanalysis into existence resolved a conflict afflicting its creator, and that psychoanalysis symbolised a personal catastrophe which had inevitably seeped into the construction of the theoretical edifice. I will reiterate Nicolas Abraham's definition: "To symbolise is to exorcise trauma

by repeating it in a context which repairs it symbolically".[6] I settled down to learning German and to reading Freud with delight, with Barbro Sylwan. We started
with Dora, whose analysis Freud began in 1900.

Fragment of an Analysis of a Case of Hysteria[7] is generally considered the text
in which Freud founded the theory of transference, describing the symptoms as
recreations of childhood events. The text did present such recreations, but we
saw added to them the traces left by Freud's relation with Fliess, a relation broken off a few weeks before Ida Bauer(alias Dora) consulted Freud. The accusa-
tions made against Dora, with supporting evidence—of homosexuality, incest and
masturbation—were caricatural reproductions of the last letters exchanged by the
two friends. They reproduced the inquisitorial nature of Fliess' observations and
Freud's passion in trying to convince his friend of the correctness of his hypotheses. As for transference, we were struck by the characteristics in Freud's attitude
towards his young patient that resembled those of Fliess, the inquisitor. Today, I
would say that what we saw was the sign of the incorporation of the traits of the
loved being Fliess had been for Freud. The work Barbro Sylwan and I did together
resulted in an article entitled "Dora between Fliess and Freud", published in 1978
and included in our book *Freud, Fliess, Ferenczi*.

Barbro and I—we had become friends—both read Freud's texts enthusiastically.
We presented the fruits of this happy labour in a seminar held within the framework
of the project "Confrontations", founded by René Major, which brought together
analysts not wishing to be locked in institutional fortresses. What the two of us
were studying was the context of the foundation of psychoanalytic theory before
and after the 1897 turning point. We read Wilhelm Fliess' books and articles, as
well as the unfavourable reviews they received from journalists in the *Wiener kli-
nische Rundschau*, the Viennese medical journal. At the same time, we were reading *The Interpretation of Dreams*, where we discovered that in his dreams Freud
agreed with these critics, while by day he continued to support and praise the man
who was his "audience of one"; the only reader of the masterpiece being elaborated. At the time, Fliess was also the doctor who treated Freud's nasal troubles. In
hindsight, I see that I was not the only one to follow a double path. As an Indian
wise man might have said: "When you come to a fork in the road, don't hesitate to
take both paths."

Barbro Sylwan and I looked closely at censure: first that imposed by Fliess and
then that carried out by the editors of the correspondence between the two friends,
published in 1950. Reading Max Schur, Freud's physician, had already informed us
of the surgery Fliess performed on Emma Eckstein's nose in February 1895, with
disastrous consequences. Schur had been able to consult the Freud archives and
to publish fragments of Freud's letters to Fliess. Thanks to him, we could picture
Freud the man: a man who strove to reassure his friend Fliess, who almost caused
Emma Eckstein's death by forgetting a length of gauze in her nasal cavity, and
who, in the months that followed, obstinately refused to recognise his mistake and
went so far as to ask Freud to interrogate Emma and blame the hemorrhage on her
hysteria.

When Freud's complete correspondence to Fliess was published by the secretary of the Freud archives, Jeff Masson, who had eluded the watchful eye of the director, Kurt Eissler, we were able to witness a formidable intellectual adventure *in statunascendi*, with its daring, its advances and retreats, its secrets big and small. We also had the elements we needed to grasp the energy our forerunners expanded to erase all traces of the traumatic in Freud's process, and the efforts they made to endow him with heroic stature. We had at our disposal the chronicle of the first psychoanalytic association composed of two members, Freud and Fliess, and this chronicle showed that those who went before us had felt obliged to censure the account of his first association, making it impossible for a time to understand what drive theory—the ontology of drives—symbolised. The influence of one of the two members of the first association had been blacked out. When the complete correspondence was finally published, it became possible to place *The Interpretation of Dreams* in a clearer light. Once the censure was lifted, the tale of the kettle made sense:

> [A] man was charged by one of his neighbours with having given him back a borrowed kettle in a damaged condition. The defendant asserted first, that he had given it back undamaged; secondly, that the kettle had a hole in it when he borrowed it; and thirdly, that he had never borrowed a kettle from his neighbour at all.[8]

We were also enlightened as to the meaning of the *Witz* in the story about the blacksmith and the tailors, often associated with the kettle story:

> There is a similar comic story of a Hungarian village in which the blacksmith had been guilty of a capital offence. The burgomaster, however, decided that as a penalty a *tailor* should be hanged and not the blacksmith, because there were two tailors in the village but no second blacksmith, and the crime must be expiated.[9]

This correspondence also revealed the quasi-systematic censure of Yiddish words and words in dialect. Restoring them contributed to the reconstruction of some painful events in Freud's childhood: the arrest in 1865 and sentencing in 1866 of Sigmund's favourite uncle for passing false rubles, a family trauma already under study by Barbro Sylwan and Maria Torok. Sigmund's childhood in Vienna became tangible, while the figure of his father lost its luster, to become that of a *Luftmensch*, an object of shame for the sons who ensured the family's survival. The direction taken by this research led us to Sigmund's half-brothers in Manchester, where we sought to understand the lifestyle of Emmanuel and Philip Freud, the ones who sent money to Vienna. We looked through telephone directories in the archives of the London Postal Service to find the names of the businesses and shops owned by the Freuds; we walked along the streets of Manchester and Newport, but could neither confirm nor deny the hypothesis we shared with Maria Torok that the brothers were involved in the uncle's trafficking of counterfeit bills made in England, as diplomatic sources suggest.

In retrospect, I tell myself that we contributed, before Ferenczi's work was published, to restoring the traumatic dimension that made Freud the first psychoanalyst. When he spoke at a meeting of *Entre-Temps*, Pierre Delaunay did not hesitate to say, speaking of psychoanalysts: "We are all war-wounded." Notwithstanding his genius, Freud became one of us, not so different from us.

Today, I sometimes think that my analysis only started then, after several years of practice. In hindsight, I became an expert on Freud in order to escape from an analytic trap that I had set up blindly, a trap reminiscent of that of my childhood—in short, in order to become a psychoanalyst. At the time, I tried my best to live up to what I was called upon to do. The only drawback was that I felt the analysands who trusted me had been better analysed than I.

We reached the 1980s. After I went through some personal crises and made a few crucial encounters, my analysis made a significant leap forward and my research took a new direction. A major change in my life was the start of a productive period in which many openings became available. This upheaval also changed the nature of the analyses I was asked to conduct. The patients were the same, but not the analyst. For the analyst I was becoming as I went through one crisis after another, analytic practice and trauma were intertwined, and the expression "trauma therapy" became a redundancy. All analytic practice was trauma therapy.

I soon joined a group of analysts formed by Pierre Delaunay, with Radmila Zygouris, Lucien Mélèse and a few others. They had voted against the arbitrary dissolution of the École freudienne de Paris (Freudian School of Paris). These analysts—a body of resistance, in fact—founded the *Fédération des ateliers de psychoanalyse* (Federation of Psychoanalytic Workshops), and I joined their ranks.

How to become a psychoanalyst? Thanks to my careful reading of the work of Nicolas Abraham and Maria Torok, I learned to recognise what Pierre Delaunay called "inverted transference". Until then, the transference I had been taught to recognise was that of the analysand's childhood feelings towards his parents onto the analyst. The concept of inverted transference, in which the analysand repeats a scene where he plays the role of the parent, while the analyst finds himself in the role of the small child, fundamentally changed my practice and unblocked stalemates. When I say "unblocked", I am speaking of making it possible to analyse not only relatively tolerable situations, but also those in which the unimaginable and unimagined emerges in deeds, in moments of crisis, on the edge of a break. The unimagined came through in my sensations and my feelings, as well as in my fantasies and dreams. It was up to me to interpret them. In my role as analyst, I had to learn to withstand periods when I was vilified, sent packing, despised. I learned to let myself be used, to be the object of a new attempt at symbolisation of the childhood trauma. I learned to bear it, to re-enact it, to enter the scene where I was summoned by the analysand and his relations—the "Six Characters in Search of an Author"[10] Luigi Pirandello introduced to us. Psychoanalysis, like theatre, requires physical fitness because the tyrant, the cruel superego, is not easily vanquished. He fights to the death to defend himself.

About Harold Searles... An exceptional translator. *The Effort to Drive the Other Person Crazy*—what a title for an article! I met him at a meeting organised in his honour by Paul-Claude Recamier, André Green and Jean-Bertrand Pontalis. Searles presented a text in which he spoke of being jealous of a schizophrenic patient— a woman—who had entrusted herself to the care of the team at Chestnut Lodge. After his presentation, an intern had been asked to describe a clinical situation where a patient is admitted to a psychiatric institution for clinical supervision. The intern talked mostly about administrative matters and diagnosis. What I remember best is Searles' reaction. He simply said to all those present what he had felt during the presentation: it had cut off his arms, given him a headache and almost put him to sleep. It had "killed him". There was nothing else to say. In hindsight, I think of the disdain the organisers of the meeting showed Searles by not supervising the young intern's clinical work. I translated, for the journal *Revue du collège de psychanalystes*, an article that Searles wrote when he started out, which had been refused by the journal of the IPA and was only published in English 30 years later.[11] In the article, Searles described how he invited his analysand to admit the part he played in causing his analyst—Searles—to act out.

When I met Françoise Davoine[12] and Jean-Max Gaudillère in 1992, I found strong allies. They shed light on concepts like *folie à deux*, plural body, the analyst and the patient who take turns being actor and spectator for each other; the person gone mad who becomes the therapist of his parent—most often one who thinks he is perfectly well. These concepts expressed in novel terms what I had learned from Ferenczi and Abraham: the theory of symbols, dual unity, the figures of the phantom and the crypt, the sense of reality. I found new support to reinforce the foundations I had acquired on my own. I never again lost them. Freud and Lacan had constructed the tools needed to conceive the physiology of representation and of repression. With them, we had been able to explore the context of the unconscious– preconscious dimension. Now, our task was to reflect on the conditions making it possible to work with that which had not taken place, which occurred but did not have someone to happen to. These tools existed as well, we just had to refine them. From then on, in the transferential relation, paradoxical demands that seemed to attack the analytic link between the analysand and myself were recognised and addressed differently. They did not come from the analysand, but from someone he had swallowed in an effort to save his feet. But in this orgiastic abandon, he lost all support, as Oedipus had. For a long time, I did not know that the French words *appui* and *s'appuyer* come from the Latin *podos*, meaning "foot". In English, "support" comes from the Latin *supportare*, to "carry from below".

My translating skills could no longer rely simply on a crossword solver's talent (I remember that Lacan advised a young analyst to do crossword puzzles); I was now called upon, first and foremost, to translate what I felt in the sessions. Everything I experienced, everything that was strange or strange to me, everything that took my breath away and astonished me had to be put into words. It was a way to bring into existence, to represent, what had been unrepresented—unrepresentable, what had not presented itself. It had not appeared either because an event had been disavowed by a witness who vanished, or because the ego was chased away by the violence of the shock.

I then took Kafka as a teacher. I don't know how he signaled to me one day from my bookcase, where his books had been sleeping for ten years. All I know is that my initial wonderment was redoubled, and that a real encounter took place. Kafka's texts were unending variations on the traumatic, on the aporetic foundation of life, its vicissitudes, its accidents and the attempts of his characters to construct makeshift foundations, or some kind of substitute support. Kafka's Ulysses, alone on his ship, tied to the mast by a flimsy tether, was able to confront more frightening Sirens than Homer's—silent Sirens. How did he resist? By pretending he didn't see them. Unlike Homer's Ulysses who asked his men to tighten his bonds when he heard the irresistible singing, in the absence of a system of seduction and abstinence, Kafka's Ulysses invented a song that did not exist, *as well as* the negation of this absence of seduction.

The seminar I gave on Kafka's work for several years led to the writing of the book *From Freud to Kafka*.[13] Today, I understand Kafka's haiku-like aphorism: "A cage went in search of a bird." I understand the cage to be the parent who had a child in order to bring himself to life. Such a child finds himself in a kind of prison with open doors.

> It was a cage. Indifferent, sovereign, the clamour of the world streamed in through the gate familiarly, the prisoner was actually free, [...] nothing outside was lost for him, he could even leave his cage, as a matter of fact the bars were several meters apart, he wasn't even captive.[14]

Kafka prompted me to read Winnicott. His work was firmly rooted in paradox.[15] How had I been dissuaded from reading him for so many years? It must have been the influence of the hostility of most SPP analysts, and Maria Torok's reserve towards him.

Many of my elders, as I said, considered Winnicott's work a maternally-inclined deviation from Freud's. They could not get past the famous proposition: "Every child is a budding Oedipus." This hypothesis which neglects the parental context, not only the maternal one, lends itself to misunderstanding. It had occasioned a revolution in Freud's thought — and the allusion came from Fliess, incidentally. This famous hypothesis, along with drive theory and psychic bisexuality, formed a system that could explain all psychic phenomena. But Freud had gone beyond the fascination to which he had originally succumbed in 1900. In 1923, in *The Ego and the Id*, as he was developing his doctrine "beyond the pleasure principle", he extracted from the Oedipus complex what I consider to be his principle—the injunction to the son: "Be like your father" and: "You may not be like your father".

Winnicott has the great merit of having closely associated this figure of the paradox—which I recognise as the core of the Oedipus complex—with its psycho-corporal origin. It goes back to a time when the infant is free to get accustomed to the paradoxical situation in which he created the mother's breast, which she provides, offering it but not giving it to him. "Where is the father in all this?", you will ask. My answer is that the paternal agency, the father in the anasemic sense of the word, is inscribed—or not—in the mother. This inscription in her explains that she does not give the infant the breast but presents it so she can create it.

Oedipus, to come back to him, is uneducable. When analysts dragged and perhaps still drag patients into a forced Oedipal march, when they relentlessly push patients who were subjected to soul murder into "oedipianisation", they add to the list of analyses where "nothing is happening" that Winnicott and Abraham, among others, criticised. By conducting such analyses, they provide justification to resolute detractors of psychoanalysis, who author articles and books in a range of tones, including "black". This insistence on Oedipus at all costs leads either to the breaking off of the analysis or the reproduction, by scissiparity, of carriers of the "virus" of psychoanalysis where "nothing is happening".

But I was not through with Oedipus. In 1994, I organised with Claude Dubarry, Georg Garner and Lucien Mélèse a conference dedicated to Jean-Joseph Goux and his book *Oedipus, Philosopher*.[16] Goux enlightened us about Oedipus' place in the great initiation monomyth of Perseus, Theseus and Bellerophon. Oedipus has his place in this monomyth—but in its monstrous version. Perseus, Theseus and Bellerophon are, each in his turn, condemned to die by a persecutory king, asked by a commissioning king to accomplish feats, and finally able to claim a fiancée promised by donating king. On the contrary, in the monstrous variant—the myth of Oedipus—there is only one king who is both persecutory and the hero's father. There is no trophy, no fiancée, no warrior's test; there is only one challenge which tests intelligence. Perseus is the name to be given to the infant who endured no psychic agony. He spent long days with Danae, who loved him; he had the support of his father, Zeus; and he was protected by Athena and Hermes, who give him the weapons the hero used to trick the Graeae and cut off Medusa's head. Later, he would free Andromeda from the monster to whom she had been promised, and marry her himself. As for Oedipus, it is a name to be reserved for the one subjected to a split in his being.

Today I see the relation between "The Vulture"[17]—Kafka's text so familiar to me by now, and on which I commented in greatest detail—and Oedipus. Today I can name Kafka's hero, who is eaten by the vulture:

A vulture was hacking at my feet It had already torn my boots and stockings to shreds, now it was hacking at the feet themselves.[18]

Today I can name the man with his feet hacked to bits, defenceless against a vulture who attacks him, and who is finally freed when the monster inexorably drowns in his blood, "which was filling ever depth, flooding ever shore." I can give him his true name: Oedipus. Oedipus swallowed the monster, the Sphinx or vulture, and acquired extraordinary intelligence. He is like the deputy minister about whom Clemenceau said: "He knows everything and nothing else." "Nothing else" because he is cut off from his body, which has stored the memory of the soul murder perpetrated against him:

> Not only emotionally, but also intellectually, can the trauma bring to maturity a part of the person. The fear of the uninhibited, almost mad adult changes the child, so to speak, into a psychiatrist.[19]

Oedipus is the hero who is cut off from himself, from the unimaginable catastrophe which left his soul—the other in him—for dead. In soul murder, who died, if not the other in the self? Emmanuel Levinas' proposition that "the soul is the other in me" reconciles me with the idea that for the psychotic there is no transference. In the sense that Freud understood transference, this idea is right, because Oedipus has stopped expecting anything from anyone. He does everything himself. He wants nothing to do with the other, and at the same time he expects all the answers from psychoanalysis. In this paradoxical transference, he expects everything from the analyst while he rejects everything that comes from him. All and nothing. This creates a situation of combat. You have to be physically fit, and love the sleeping child, the bird in the cage. Once the vulture is identified, I name him and describe his strategy. Things become more complicated because the child in the patient is acquainted with the child left for dead in the parent, and he loves that child, although the adult parent is a monster.

Oedipus' intelligence is remarkable, as his "I" is cut off from his ego. His fetish object is intelligence. He is not supported by the absent third party, who always renews the questioning, connecting life *and* death. It is not in the other that he finds the support he needs not to lose ground, because when he lost his feet, he lost the ability to lean on another. In his psychic torment, he forgot how to count to three, and since then he roams in the land of "all or nothing", between counterparts to incest and murder. Oedipus is the hero of the hidden traumatic break, the paradigm of catastrophic healing.

Oedipus is the model hero because he has been subjected to trauma. What is trauma? An impossible-to-remember event that went unnoticed because it changed the subject of the experience. What signals trauma is loss of the ability to be surprised by the existence of the world, and of the striving to find an explanation where we are expected to see the facts as a "primitive phenomenon."[20] Oedipus has no questions left, only answers.

How does one become a psychoanalyst? I had spent many years exploring the question of soul murder, I had written a book about it, and I had yet to discover that I did not know the most important thing—that I too was an Oedipus (although not budding) because, like the deputy minister, I knew nothing else. I was learning it in the transference, in a manner painful for my self-esteem, by repeating the crime I did not want to know had been committed against me. These analyses allowed me to access the ruins which I thought had only been discovered by Kafka, Celan and a few analysands. I was grateful to these analysands for having forced me to go so far—Pierre Delaunay speaks of symbolic constraint—for having forced me to recognise the reciprocity of the transference; for inciting me to talk about these things that can only be told to one person at a time, provided, as a wiseman in the Talmud says, that that person already knows these things at least as well as you do.

Notes

1 Sylwan, B. and Réfabert, P., *Freud, Fliess, Ferenczi. Des fantômes qui hantent la psychanalyse*, Paris, Hermann, 2010.
2 Laplanche, J. and *Pontalis*, J.-B., "Fantasy and the Origins of Sexuality", *International Journal of Psychoanalysis*, 1968, 49: 1–18.
3 Ferenczi, S., "Confusion of the Tongues between the Adults and the Child", *The International Journal of Psychoanalysis*, 30: 225–230, 1949.
4 Réfabert, P., "Désaveu, abjuration"[Disavowal, Repudiation], *Revue française de psychanalyse*, 39(3), 1975.
5 Torok, M., *Le Coq-Héron*, 159, 2000.
6 Abraham, N. and Torok, M., *The Shell and the Kernel*, Chicago, University of Chicago Press, 1994.
7 Freud, S., *Fragment of an Analysis of a Case of Hysteria*, S.E. 7: 1–122, London: Hogarth.
8 Freud, S., *The Interpretation of Dreams*, S.E. 4: 1–338, London: Hogarth.
9 Freud, S., *Jokes and Their Relation to the Unconscious*, S.E. 8: 9–236, London: Hogarth.
10 Pirandello, L., *Six Characters in Search of an Author*, New York, Dover Publications, 1997.
11 Searless, H., "Concerning Transference and Countertransference" (1949), *Revue du Collège de psychanalystes*, 48, 1994.
12 Davoine, F., *Wittgenstein's Folly*, New York, YBK Publishers, 2012.
13 Réfabert, P., *From Freud to Kafka*, London, Karnac Books, 2014.
14 Kafka, F., *Wedding Preparations in the Country and Other Prose from the Estate*, Frankfurt, M. Fischer Taschenbuch Verlag, 1983.
15 Winnicott, D. W., *Playing and Reality*, Oxford, Routledge Classics, 1971.
16 Goux, J-J., *Oedipus, Philosopher*, Redwood City, CA, Stanford University Press, 1994.
17 Kafka, F., *The Complete Stories*, New York, Schocken Books, 1995.
18 Kafka, F., *The Complete Stories*, New York, Schocken Books, 1971.
19 Ferenczi, S., "Confusion of the Tongues Between the Adults and the Child", *art. cit.*, p. 229.
20 Hadot, P., *Wittgenstein et les limites du langage*, Paris, Vrin, 2015, p.71.

Preface

Olivier Paccoud

It is a joy and an honour for me to write the Preface to Philippe Réfabert's book. A joy because for the past few years I have been saddened to know that these remarkable texts were dispersed here and there—since, in my work as an analyst, I had occasion to discover their critical importance. I am therefore very happy that their author has agreed to have them brought together in the present work. These texts cover a period of about 20 years; they show the reader the road travelled by Philippe Réfabert and the stages that gradually led to the hypotheses he developed in his previously published works.

In preparing the present collection, we strove to preserve the coherence and fluidity of the texts included. In truth, this was an easy task, thanks to the depth of a reflection built on extremely rich views that allowed it to expand and open onto new horizons.

It was also an honour, as I said, since I believe that these texts can be considered essential contributions to psychoanalytic literature. In my experience, there are few analytic writings that focus so directly on analysis; on the analytic endeavour itself. We keep such writings close at hand and draw on them often to renew the early enthusiasm worn away by the practice of this "impossible profession", as Freud called it. Whenever we return to them, we have the impression of discovering psychoanalysis for the first time, as if all at once it was possible to converse again with this other language in our own language.

My experience with analytic literature has rarely given me the feeling of hearing such a unique voice, so decidedly singular and clear as Philippe Réfabert's. What is more, I have rarely met an analyst who has ventured so far, with such obstinacy, into psychoanalytic territory, and so, inevitably, into its margins. Finally, and not surprisingly, rarely have I read such a disturbing and far from consensual analyst. Perhaps what makes an analyst is, after all, the unique and disturbing language he has created and lets us hear. This language has an untranslatable quality, an essence that cannot be transposed to another idiom. Philippe Réfabert's language—his voice, to be more exact—speaks to us from the eminently exceptional place where psychoanalysis invents itself. Such voices always remind us of that aspect of psychoanalysis which is strictly untransmissible. Knowing this, reading these texts cannot fail to unsettle us and move us deeply. They touch something in us that we didn't know was there, show us that we have left the safety of our certainties; they wake us from our "dogmatic slumber", to use Kant's expression.

It will not come as a surprise, then, to detect in these texts a certain mistrust with regard to mainstream psychoanalysis or the teaching of the established schools. Nor is it a surprise to see that Philippe Réfabert is very much at home with certain chosen analysts, with poets, writers and philosophers, as well as with art and theology, while writing and thinking—in short, while being an analyst.

Nor will it come as a surprise to see that in such company psychoanalysis can breathe freely, and so can we. We shall also see that in the place to which he takes analysis, where he allows analysands to lead him (to "breathlessness"), this is the only acceptable company, these are the only acceptable words—as if drawn, or pulled out if need be, of the immemorial underpinnings of language.

Because Philippe Réfabert's thinking was forged with *and* against established psychoanalytic language and, in this sense, with *and* against Freud, his book constantly invites us to maintain an ethical resistance to dogmatic psychoanalysis; I mean by this ideological psychoanalysis that casts no shadow and cannot sustain itself with the "negative capability" so dear to Bion, or with the "learned ignorance"—a term Lacan borrowed from Nicolas de Cues—which allows for no paradox. This position is close to that of Sándor Ferenczi, D.W. Winnicott, Nicolas Abraham and Maria Torok; Lacan also perhaps—in short, all those "cursed" analysts who wanted to remind their colleagues—and Freud first of all—of the true significance of his discovery. These analysts all agreed on one thing: they maintained that otherness is there from the beginning, that psychic life and the subject do not develop alone. They opposed a "solipsistic conception", as Laplanche says, of the psyche. They sometimes paid for this dearly: in his poignant introductory text, Philippe Réfabert reminds us of the high price one sometimes pays for daring to question certain founding principles of analytic theory—specifically the role of the object, of the environment and of the other in the construction of the psyche. Indeed, it was because he became alarmed early in his life at the psycho-corporal effects of "totalitarian outcroppings" in the environment, and because he built on this awareness, that he was able to turn around, regain his footing and become, little by little, the analyst he is today. His testimony is far from being simply a condemnation of this environment. His perspective—that of trauma therapy, concerned with the effects of such an environment on the psychic life of the *infans*, invites us to reflect on the inception of psychic life. This perspective renders possible a metapsychology of this environment, of an analytic practice focused on the object, and especially on what is transferred "in full force" between the object and the subject. This reveals the need for an in-depth review of drive theory rooted in naturalist ontology.[1] It follows that we need to rethink the psychic functioning of the analyst in the session, and specifically to reflect not only on countertransference but also on the analyst's transference. Finally, this testimony opens the way to psychoanalytic reflection on the history of psychoanalysis, to an analytic treatment of the theory and its transmission: we will see how and why "Oedipus complex", "drive theory" and "primary narcissism" can also be the names by which the author designates this problematic "transmission".

Philippe Réfabert considers that psychoanalysis must concern itself with acts and, I would say, with the archives of the body—"de-tested" memories that have only the body as a witness. The author holds a view of analysis in which witnessing is crucial. In his view, the analyst cannot recuse himself, but must testify. He can be witness to the ethical abandonment suffered by his analysand, but he is also, and above all, led to become witness, in the transference, to his own zones of deafness, of the fortresses behind which he keeps the parts of himself he was unable to protect; the parts "left for dead". Such an analyst risks paying an exorbitant price for the adventure he invites the analysand to undertake. Philippe Réfabert disagrees with a solipsistic conception of the psyche primarily because he feels that it unduly exculpates the object, whom we may also call "the parent"—but whose name, in this view, should also be "the psychoanalyst".

At every turn, Philippe Réfabert invites us to view the theory psychoanalytically, and contextualise it transferentially. This makes it conceivable to use the theory defensively, particularly as a fetish, in a context of catastrophic transferential resolution—conceivable, for instance, when it is urgent to hide a crime. In this case, the parent or the analyst is no longer a seducer in principle: on the contrary, the seduction takes on a traumatic character, since a witness is buried in the foundations of the original encounter, or of the theory, given that sexual phantasising is "an *ad hoc* cover, since it is considered to be the *fons et origio* of psycho-corporal life". The author maintains that, in truth, sexual fantasy should be seen as "one of the psyche-soma's preferred ways to humanise the omissions history left in the fabric of memory; one of the exquisite means of symbolising that which was not symbolised in the previous generations". It would be hard to take a clearer stance or to propose a better outcome of the false alternative at the origin of the opposition between fantasmatic causality (internal) and traumatic causality (external).

This view has a powerful impact on psychoanalytic theory: it demands, as we shall see, a reformulation of the fundamental paradigms of psychoanalysis. It also has major consequences for analytic practice and technique. Before looking more closely at the texts included here, one thing must be made clear: Philippe Réfabert's analytic conceptualisation is difficult, and even painful, because it tests our ability to bear the thought that an entire "analysis" can concern itself with an object who recants, recuses himself or has been absent; that it can be, throughout, the analysis of an "object without a shadow" which gains sway over the subject[2]—the analysis of a "thing without a name", of a "vulture" (that of Kafka) that the subject unwittingly swallowed, and with whom he constructed a "paradoxical foundation". The author forces us to see our reflection in the unflattering mirror of an "innocent" analysis, with a sphinx-like analyst well acquainted with the art of "as if it never happened", which, in the name of Oedipus, of drive theory or of mastery over the countertransference, will endlessly "repeat the crime", as Ferenczi pointed out. To this resignation, Philippe Réfabert opposes a witness-analyst, an analyst willing to let himself be reached, to "suffer the other" and to carry, for instance, a hatred he did not know he felt towards his analysand. Such an analyst could testify to "soul murder" which, strictly speaking, has not yet taken place, for it never found its place. By taking psychoanalysis in this direction, specifically towards the infamous path of mutual analysis Philippe Réfabert places it, once again, on paths both fascinating and disquieting. Reading these texts reminds us that this is, indeed, a "dangerous method",[3] and therefore unparalleled, for the healing of the human soul.

About the Origin

> *If all the forms of psychopathology, including hysteria, are tied—as I am suggesting—to a failing of primal repression, then the entire axiomatic body of psychoanalysis deserves to be rebuilt on foundations better able to account for phenomena close to the origin. In other words, we are talking about changing the paradigm through which we view psychoanalysis.*
>
> "About a Limit Not Established at the Outset", *infra*.

As this introductory quotation indicates, the chapters comprising Part I of the book concern the question of the origin in psychoanalysis, and the conditions and aims of its repression. My intention is to explain to what extent, and in what theoretical areas, Philippe Réfabert's conception—relative to these two questions—renders certain axiomatic foundations of psychoanalysis ill-adjusted, or outright unusable. Following the example set by Ferenczi, Balint, Bion and Winnicott, the author proposes an "intersubjective" conception of the origins, of the foundation of the subject, and thereby opens the possibility of considering the conditions in which psychoanalysis was created. This also makes it possible to tell the story of the application of the theory, with its failures, impasses and catastrophes. Indeed, subjectivity cannot emerge from a closed system (primary narcissism), as an agreement-in-principle (primary repression), without creating a major epistemological obstacle. If the child's inner being is delimited at the origin, any articulation between the metapsychology of the origins and transference causality becomes impossible. In the sphere of the origins, Philippe Réfabert attaches great importance to Winnicott's concept of transitionality, considered consubstantial with the foundation of the subject. By introducing the concepts of transitional psychic matrix and rhythmic concertation, the author invites us to conceive of the origins of the subject as transitional (paradoxical) and rhythmic.

The psychic matrix is the semiotic envelope offered by the mother—"found/created" by the child, through which he makes contact with the world. Like Bion, Philippe Réfabert asserts that the mother dreams the child and can only meet the "real" child "in the mirror of this matricial child". On his part, the child adjusts to this protective matrix when dealing with his first sensations: the child can only experience what he feels if he was first "savoured"; "intuited" in the matricial mirror created by the mother. The author asserts that within this matrix each event is given a positive *and* negative value: events are good and bad, subjective and objective, internal and external; these events can henceforth exist and endure on a transitional level of undecidability. A "good enough" mother will guarantee this transitional envelope and the indeterminate status of the infant's experiences (of finding/creating). The author adds that a "good enough" mother who can "take death upon herself" can therefore give the gift of human discontinuity. Because she herself will benefit or has benefited from a facilitating environment, she can manage her failings, identify them and indicate where they are. A mother who is in possession of her own death (who does not expect her child to keep her alive) can "give the shadow" and by doing so is ready to delimit, to detect the unknowable. She can transmit the negative and, consequently, become the child's "adversary": by allowing him to turn against her (ad-versum), she turns him away from the shortest path—that of extinction, indifference, nothingness.

In describing this essential contribution made by Philippe Réfabert, I find it very important to emphasise that the transitional psychic matrix is rhythmic. The matrix is located at the intersection of force and meaning: structurally it gives a "yes-and-no" in which "yes-and-no" are rhythmically connected within a "rhythmic concertation". In this context, rhythmicity guarantees the potential strength of the matrix and its polarisation; it also provides the conditions needed for introjection of drives adjusted to the child's rhythm. The function of the psychic matrix is to maintain and sustain, to contain and connect, aporetic dualities: incitation/restraint and continuity/discontinuity. A child, as well as an analysand, who can build upon and rely on this matrix for support once it has been introjected, has also received the capacity to withstand discontinuity. The introjected transitional psychic matrix functions like a primary container, a system of rhythmic intensities which will in-sure, throughout life, the capacity for transition, that is, the ability to go to through life crises without breaking down. Near the origins, on the other hand, the *Neben-mensch*[4]—as well as the analyst—cannot do without an active presence able to sus-tain the rhythmic concertation: "The only adequate answer to dizziness is rhythm", the author cites Henri Maldiney as saying. It is in view of this requirement that I understand Philippe Réfabert's insistence on the need for practicing hemostasis, even a "teaching the territory": the terrain of the analysis is often far from clear, and it requires the presence of a vigilant and attentive analyst who can be entrusted with the fragile, rhythmic phrases whose emergence analysis can make possible.

Seen in this light, the psychic matrix is akin to the transitional umbilicus of our subjectivity. Being supported by its paradoxical consistency allows us to make the unfathomable a solid foundation, to "inhabit the paradoxical space of living-and-dying". Conversely, Philippe Réfabert also asks us to imagine the consequences, for subjectivity, of an inadequate original transitional space. If the matrix has blind spots, or dead or hemorrhagic zones, there will be parallel dead, frightened or inert zones in the infant's psyche. Near the origins, "antirhythmic caesuras" as Hölderlin called them, will provoke radical symptomatic responses in the infant's psyche-soma: "catastrophic healing" is Réfabert's eloquent term, borrowed from Jean Paulhan. The subject, dislodged from his foundations ("when the shipwreck causes splitting, the split is a new foundation"), will have to find support not in a "division", as Lacan understands it, but in a break—a split. To survive, he will have to invent a vicarious—rather than transitional—paradox, but a "crafty" one: a new subject can then emerge, on the very site of the catastrophe, where it will be both founded and subsumed, as well as cut off from itself. This vicarious "foundation" will prove to be the "place" of a specific memory, that of the agony, the splitting; an unremembered catastrophe in which fracture, like an arrhythmic failing, stands in the place of a memory to come.

Philippe Réfabert describes the subject of trauma as a subject who cannot face the "between-the-lines" (the trace of death). The concept of a psyche that associates, based on repression theory, does not apply to him; in practice, I believe he forces the analyst to confront the limits of the "classical" technique based on free association. The subject the author refers to is "stunned"—that is, inaccessible, out of reach; he has gotten away. But he is just as much petrified, knocked out, "left for dead". Given these premises, primary narcissism can no longer be taken for granted. At the clinical level, "primary survival" solutions are more likely—enacted as deadly "narcissistic" functioning, manipulative, aiming to exclude the other radically, *in order to* maintain an interaction with him. The "stupefied" subject the author portrays will deploy enormous energy in the search for a "purified", totalitarian psycho-corporal organisation casting no shadow. Constantly haunted by a "thing-without-a-name", he will strive tirelessly, *at the same time*, to take the shape of an object that escapes detection. Such a subject will always be impelled to establish "all or nothing" relations.

More generally, placing the other, the *Nebenmensch*, at the centre of primary narcissism makes it inevitable to examine the extremely complex stakes at play in his history, and the paradoxical figures of its historisation. Here, Philippe Réfabert disagrees with Freud (a certain Freud, to be sure). He distinguishes himself even more radically from analysts who consider the problem of primary narcissism to have been solved when the subject was structurally endowed with original closure, with a theoretical transitional psychic matrix. Based on this supposition, these analysts believe the subject to possess the ability to turn back on himself—to conduct his own subjective trial—without going mad and without killing himself.[5] Such analysts assume that despite certain resistances these analysands are able to turn back on themselves, and therefore to "play" with the device of the analysis. In my view, they underestimate the founding paradox of original narcissism, which cannot be conceived subjectively "with no problem" unless it runs into a problem.

Philippe Réfabert acquaints us with the idea that the subject is not born equipped with a paradoxical system enabling him to counterinvest the void, or indifference. Turning away from the worst is not something one can do alone (or only at an exorbitant cost). A subject forced to give himself a paradoxical foundation for being finds himself in the position of an amateur mountain climber who has been "teletransported" to the top of the mountain by means of a psychic substitutive system of survival. It follows that "clinical practice conducted by an analyst solely from the perspective of sexual difference could be compared to the landscape discovered at the top of the mountain by a climber brought there by helicopter" (see infra.). An analysis conducted on such a basis would lead to a denial of splitting. It would repeat the rejection, leaving the child in the analysand at the same time here—at the foot of the mountain, in suspense, in the waiting room of his story; and there—at the summit, not knowing that he put himself there by sacrificing one of his vital functions.

According to Philippe Réfabert, where the unthinkable has to be disavowed, and this disavowal is redoubled in analysis, all that is left are bodily signs (dizziness, dysfunction, panic).

They are the ultimate witnesses to an unspeakable catastrophe which will henceforth disrupt time and space. This is an understatement when you've been turned upside down, when you're in "the fourth dimension", when you dream with your eyes open. Réfabert's "catastrophic healing" child, who used a fetish to construct a vicarious mirror in an emergency—a substitute for a matrix—is a child who was "de-possessed" of a transfixing, primitive mirror. In other words, the mirror in which he reflects himself, which sustains his identity, is also a rear-view mirror reflecting future anguish. This child, who was unable to see himself, to learn who he is, in the mirror of his mother's face, was confronted instead with a mother striving to see *herself* in her child (here, the author reverses our common perspective on projective identification). Such a mother, cut off from her origins, attempts to find her reflection, to re-anchor herself, by clinging to her child's body. A child, a "wise baby", as Ferenczi called him, "stuck" with this terrifying task, will have to deal with being the physical locus of a catastrophe to come—undetectable, a "thing without a name" from a past his mother does not know she has.

Witnessing: "As if it never happened"

What I am going to propose here is that psychoanalytic treatment be considered from the perspective of witnessing. [...] It has occurred to me that this perspective is worth expanding to the whole range of psychopathologies, and that it would be useful to see analysis as the experience in which an analyst creates conditions allowing the witness in the analysand to see that he has recovered his ability to testify for himself and for the other.

Philippe Réfabert, "The Witness, Subject of the Psychoanalysis", *infra.*

The texts composing Part II of the book examine psychoanalytic theory and practice from the perspective of witnessing. The "witness" becomes a tool for the author, a viewpoint[6] suited to the treatment of trauma—as he sees it and advocates it. In this context, the author's interlocutor of choice, after Kafka, is Paul Celan, an ally in the attempt to grasp the consequences of such a paradigm when applied to psychoanalysis. At the clinical level, this perspective has radical implications: if "Celan's battle is fought against the forgetting of the forgetting of unthinkable anguish, or, in metapsychological terms, against the forgetting of original repression" (see infra.), a witness may have to ground himself in the place of the other, on a vertiginous "I/you remember". At the theoretical level, such a perspective would encourage psychoanalysis, and particularly Freudian teaching, not to start with abstract dehistoricised founding principles, but with life-size contextual frames of articulation: "We agreed very quickly, [Barbro Sylwan and I] to focus our research not on the well-known foundations of this great edifice [the Freudian œuvre], but on the catastrophes that this monumental edifice symbolises and of which it is the trace".[7]

I am going to identify three distinct areas in which, thanks to witnessing, Philippe Réfabert raises what I consider to be essential questions for psychoanalysis. First, the witnessing perspective allows clinical questioning of the foundations of psychoanalysis—an interpretation, and even an analytic elaboration of certain original scenes of analytic theory. Given my very limited competence in the history of psychoanalysis, I will not venture to discuss the author's hypotheses based on his research and the historical facts he collected: specifically about Freud's relationship with Fliess. However, I am extremely interested in the intension the author pursues in his investigations, be it that of the trio Freud/Fliess/Eckstein; or the 1930 conflict between Freud and Ferenczi—this intention being to recreate the context, to portray and animate the intersubjective, transferential background which led to the theory, and from which certain fundamental principles emerge.

In fact, the author invites us to conceive of certain founding elements of analytic doctrine as sweeping catastrophic resolutions (conceptually brilliant *because* they are catastrophic); of transferential relation at an impasse, involving traumatic zones in the protagonists. Because Fliess refuses to accept responsibility for Emma Eckstein's botched surgery[8] (Philippe Réfabert calls him a "man without a shadow"); because Freud (the Freud of that period, at least) cannot oppose the Fliess who offers him the unconditional protection of an ideal mother; and finally because Emma, who "symbolises with the very thing that is killing her", cannot lodge a direct complaint and call her aggressor into question, all three of them introduce a faulty witness in the foundations of psychoanalysis. Moreover, the birth of psychoanalysis is also founded on soul murder[9] if, as the author suggests, "the misrepresentation of the dream about the Emma affair as a dream princeps, and the concept of a budding Oedipus at the core of the child—with the dual instinct theory correlative to it—makes it possible to shield a witness who refuses to testify". The Emma affair and the 1930 crisis involving Freud and Ferenczi, as presented by the author, appear to be unfinished enquiries—because a particular witness is not heard, or another refuses to testify. Philippe Réfabert speaks of the "childhood illness of psychoanalysis" to designate this theoretical sequestration of fractures no one wanted to assume. When "the pot of metapsychology is pierced by a seducer who is a concealed defaulting witness", what is created is a shadowless psychoanalysis forgetful of its ethics: a psychoanalysis which will inevitably replace the requirement of bearing witness with Presence ontology.

I will comment more briefly on the second question examined from the perspective of witnessing: the review and complexification of the original stakes involved in the birth of the subject. We have seen that Philippe Réfabert considers it essential that in the sphere of the origins there be a rhythmic matrix that can transitionally frame, contain and reflect the exchanges between the mother and the infant—without assigning them a specific place. In this perspective, the mother is the main actor, the witness of choice and the guardian of this matricial field, of this "alpha-betisation" (Ferro[10]) of the earliest sensations: "A sensation comes into being provided the child finds in his environment a witness who makes himself the messenger between his body and his psyche". Thus, the witness anticipates, prefigures as it were, thanks to a kind of creative—but never saturated—intuition,[11] the rhythmic possibilities of the other, the capacity the child will develop later to sustain creatively, by becoming a witness himself, the relation between his "I" and his "ego". The witnessing perspective also overturns our conception of primal fantasies: it discredits the abstract, theoretical parents that the doctrine imagines for the child, as well as the ready-made fantasies it attributes to him. This perspective invites us to question these primal "transcendental" fantasies in general, and the private makeshift systems a subject constructs to compensate the inadequate foundations of his identity. Indeed, in trauma therapy, the witness will always be more or less inadequate: he will always leave it to the child to deal with a "thing without a name" which covers over the trace of death. This makes it possible to imagine a therapy that deals with failures, with losses, and even the betrayal or destruction of the witness. The central element in such a therapy is soul murder: "As soon as the witness is rendered powerless, the subject loses his balance, primal repression is destroyed and mends itself extemporaneously at the expense of the Ego; that is, the child creates in a flash—all creation is instantaneous—a *new subject*, a *prosthetic subject*, by inventing a neo-primal repression on the spot". He accomplishes this rescue operation by negating a part of himself, which he substitutes for the missing negation.

The third divergence consists of seeing the treatment itself as an act of witnessing: "To answer the question: 'what is a psychoanalyst?' we can now say that it is someone who is willing to be called upon to confirm a certain trauma, a certain aspect of the real that an analysand—a particular one—feels impelled to bring to light". In this context, Philippe Réfabert examines the conditions, the aims and the modalities of witnessing, particularly in extreme transferential circumstances—when soul murder is present in the analysis—an analysis which is bound to repeat the crime. In the author's own words: "The analysis of someone who has been seduced by a blind and deaf surface, a surface without writing; and has been deprived of the psychic matrix in which a parent holds a child, with no testimony from the other parent about this omission and its effects, and nothing done to compensate for them—such an analysis will take place near the origins, near the analyst's 'rock bottom'". In this place of breathlessness, where something was dismissed without inscription, the analyst is expected to rely on his own depths to reveal Celan's "time-crevasse" into which the witness sunk—not in the analysand this time, but in the analyst. For indeed, the analysand is deflected unfailingly, like a magnetic needle, towards the deaf zones that a trauma has created in the analyst's hearing faculty: the little door of the closet where the analyst keeps the parts of himself left for dead. It is easy to see the radical nature of this perspective, and its equally radical consequences for analytic practice: it calls on the analyst to give of himself, and tests the limits of psychoanalysis (our representations of psychoanalysis) at every level. The author also insists, contrary to the somewhat naïve and comforting conception of construction in psychoanalysis, that in these situations it is out of the question to reconstitute the past by using the neutral language of "what happened"; nor is it admissible to "represent" the real on the pretext of reconciling with it. The pressing need to "move on" (in psychoanalytic language, to forgo the Oedipus or symbolic castration) risks contributing to the repetition of the rejection. I interpret what the author means here by "witnessing" as the transgressive intrusion made by an act of speech forcibly pulled out of anguish. Where breath was taken away, the analyst who dares to testify allows the event without a place to emerge as an occurrence, so that breath can return. But the analyst who ventures to utter such a word, a "counter-word" as Celan calls it, also attests to his analysand that someone has finally taken the risk of paying the cost.[12] And this really has no price.

* * *

At the heart of narcissism, at the foundation of the subject, at the origin of psychic life, there is alterity. There, in the best case, the subject has been given a transitional psychic matrix solid enough to help him, at times of crisis in his life, recover his breath and his balance and not "fall out of this world" (Grabbe, quoted by Freud). But sometimes a subject is forced to perform a complicated acrobatic manoeuvre to build a vicarious paradoxical foundation on which, no matter what happens, he can attempt to stand. This subject may have had to face the double alterity (the double alteration) of an unspeakable *jouissance* and of an object without a shadow, in an effort to give himself the negative, that is, a place. In these circumstances, psychoanalysis will be this trial, this crossing which allows the subject to bring into question the place which he believed to be his foundation. A psychoanalyst can encourage and accompany such a "catastrophic change"—Bion's term—if he is willing to lose his footing, to support himself on his depths—to testify.

In my view, this is the essential message of this book. For the benefit of readers not acquainted with Philippe Réfabert's previous work, I thought it useful to place the texts contained herein in the larger context of the author's journey and theoretical explorations. I tried to show how these texts connect with, expand and throw a different light on the previous work. This book—so vividly inhabited, and so distinctly shaped and inspired from start to finish by Kafka and Celan respectively—might have been called *From Kafka to Celan*. With Kafka's help, the author offers support to a child when the ground falls out from beneath his feet and he must instantly put in place the support Freud assumed he was given at birth.

Philippe Réfabert makes us aware of the true scope of this cataclysm, capable of overturning the order of the world. How can one testify to such a catastrophe? Philippe Réfabert's encounter with Celanwas no doubt crucial, and the effect of Celan's writings on witnessing considerable. Moreover, the spirit of Ferenczi's thought is present throughout the book. Whether we are speaking of the history of psychoanalysis, of its transmission or of what the stakes are in an analysis, Philippe

Réfabert is clearly an enfant terrible of psychoanalysis, ready to provoke the "homo psychanalyticus", as François Perrier called him, in each of us.

Above and beyond the questions and challenges set forth in this book, as well as the perspectives it opens for analytic thought and practice, I hope I have been able to indicate to what extent the book calls into question psychoanalysis as a whole, in a discerning and inspired manner. At the same time, the book sets psychoanalysis on a new course, asking it to resist that tendency in itself which rebels against its own movement, against its own objective. The author tells us that psychoanalysis cannot advance unless it insists on looking at its own foundations, constantly disturbing them, and re-examining premises that constitute limits to reflection. Thus, the identity of psychoanalysis is necessarily fluctuating, uncertain, precarious. The author asks how we can think about or rethink its transmission, given such premises (on "the tip of a paradox"). Indeed, this was one of the crucial questions at the forefront of my mind as I was reading the book.

Notes

1 Réfabert, P., *From Freud to Kafka,* London, Karnac, 2014.
2 I would like to draw attention to the many resonances between Philippe Réfabert's thought and that of René Rousillon. See: Rousillon, R. "La métaphysique des processus" [A Metaphysics of Processes], *Revue française de psychanalyse*, 59(5), 1995; or more clinical, *Agonie, clivage et symbolisation* [Agony, Splitting and Symbolisation], Paris, Presses Universitaires de France, 1999.
3 A reference to David Cronenberg's film *A Dangerous Method*, Lago Film, 2011.
4 Freud, S., *The Origins of Psycho-Analysis: Letters to Wilhelm Fliess, Drafts and Notes, 1887–1902*, New York, Basic Books, 1954.
5 On this subject, see Mélèse, L., Dubarry, C., Réfabert, P. and Garner, G., *Les travaux d'Oedipe, d'après "Oedipe philosophe" de Jean-Joseph Goux*, Paris, L'Harmattan, 1997.
6 On this subject, see De Macedo, H., "Paranoia as Seen by Philippe Réfabert", *Letters to a Young Psychoanalyst*, Oxford, Routledge, 2017.
7 Sylwan, B., and Réfabert, P., *Freud, Fliess, Ferenczi. Des fantômes qui hantent la psychanalyse*, Paris, Hermann, 2010.
8 Freud, we might recall, entrusted his patient Emma Eckstein to Fliess in February 1895 for a nose operation intended to treat stomach problems. Fliess left a length of gauze in the young woman's nasal cavity; subsequently emergency surgery was needed to remove it. Fliess never acknowledged his error.
9 "Soul murder is murder of the witness, the disappearance of the Other in oneself". "Soul murder is a thing without a name, by contrast to God, the name of names which names no thing. Rather than a name which designates nothing, what insists here is a thing which has no name". Réfabert, P., *From Freud to Kafka*, London, Karnac, 2014.
10 Antonino Ferro, *Evitare le emozioni, vivere le emozioni*, Milan, Rafaello Cortina, 2007.
11 I am indebted to Pierre-Henri Castel for this notion of creative maternal intuition, based on Wilfred Bion's thought.
12 "I do not think a patient will ever accept an interpretation, however correct, unless he feels that the analyst has passed through an emotional crisis as a part of the act of giving the interpretation". Bion, W., *Cogitations*, Oxford, Routledge, 1991.

Part I

About the Originary

In der Mandel – was steht in der Mandel?
Das Nichts.
Essteht das Nichts in der Mandel.
Da steht es und steht.
In Nichts – wersteht da? Der König.
Da steht der König, der König.
Da stehter und steht.

In the Almond – what dwells in the Almond?
Nothing.
Nothing dwells in the Almond.
There it dwells and dwells.
In Nothing, what dwells there? The King.
There dwells the King, the King.
There he dwells and dwells.

Paul Celan, "Mandorla", in *Memory Rose into Threshold Speech*,
New York, Farrar, Straus and Giroux, 2020.

DOI: 10.4324/9781003435730-1

1

About a Limit Not Given at the Origin

One day, God dreamed of not being. Of all the living creatures he had created, male and female, he chose to endow humans with speech and thereby enable them to imagine what is not. He breathed life into Man's soul and gave him the ability to conjure up that which dwells outside of presence: negation.

Until then, elements emerged from the void by virtue of His invocation, and he called them good to very good; but the category "bad" did not exist. God decided to create it specifically for Man's use, but in association with "good". God gave Man a concept that would be his alone: the "good and bad".

In the Garden of Eden where He placed Man, God planted trees which delighted the eye and were good to eat. He also planted the Tree of Life and the Tree of Knowledge, good and bad, in the garden. He did not plant a Tree of Knowledge of good and evil. No, He left that to philosophers and theologians who would insist on seeing them grow. Neither did He plant trees giving two sorts of fruit: good and bad. Instead, He planted a tree whose fruit was both good and bad. But that was not all. He commanded Man in a manner as contradictory as the fruit of this tree. In Hebrew, this verse may be read as a command to eat and not to eat of the fruit of this tree.

This double command meant that Man should eat of the fruit of the Tree of Knowledge, because he is to eat of every tree; and should not eat of it. God did not command him to eat of the fruit of every tree except the Tree of Knowledge, but rather to eat of the fruit of every tree in the garden and not to eat of the fruit of the Tree of Knowledge. This command was not a threat; it was a paradoxical command. From that moment on, humans were in a situation where they were to eat and not to eat of the fruit of the Tree of Knowledge good and bad. "Of every tree in the garden thou mayest freely eat. But of the Tree of Knowledge thou shalt not eat, for in the day that thou eatest thereof thou shalt surely die".

The fact that the word "die" is used here for the first time does not mean that until then animals did not die, or that their death was not real, but that animals receive life, while human creatures receive life-and-death; both together. Man has access to the representation of his finitude because he is the only living creature who, being endowed with speech, can perpetuate the existence of that which has disappeared from his sight. Things present themselves to animals. Man is given

DOI: 10.4324/9781003435730-2

the ability to represent them to himself. Man knows finitude, buries his dead and remembers them. He is the only living creature residing in the paradoxical space of living-and-dying. Contrary to animals, who see "the open" and what is outside, but do not perceive what is not there, humans perceive the invisible. Rainer Maria Rilke celebrates this difference:

> *With all its eyes the creature sees the Open.*
> *Only our eyes are as though reversed,*
> *and placed all around them as traps, encircling their free exit.*
> *What is outside we know only*
> *from the animal's countenance;*
> *for already we turn around the young child*
> *and force it to see backwards, see form,*
> *not the open that's so deep in the animal's face. Free of death. It, only we see.*
> *The free animal has its demise always behind it*
> *and before it God, and when it moves,*
> *it moves eternity, as the fountains move.*[1]

The gift of paradox, in the word and through the word, allows man to bring into existence what is not, in the image of God, who is not but must come forth – *Heiyeh Asher Heyieh* – not to be wrongly translated "that I be who I am", since the Hebrew verb is in the future tense, but rather "I shall be what I have to be". The gift of paradox gives Man the ability to see himself, to be at once an "I" who watches and a "me" who is seen, as well as the subject who says: "I see myself" in an internal mirror that enables him to perceive what he is not—to perceive his image. Thanks to speech, Man can tell himself a story and he can be wrong, as he pleases. He can know and not know, he can remember and forget; he can be the subject and the object of an action at the same time, as he is in the act of watching; he can be both subject—placed below—and object—placed outside. Through good and bad speech, he can take possession of magnificent singularity or forgo it in favour of another man to whom he will submit. Finally, he can see himself clearly in thought, or be wrong about who he is. But above all, this duality allows him, if need be, to undertake a process of transformation of his relation to himself.

The child is upset if he is asked whether he created his transitional object or found it among the objects around him. When asked such a question, he can neither feel nor think that he has just been brutally ousted from the potential space he was occupying, a space specific to the originary sphere where all things are at once internal and external, good and bad, and where duplicity opposes the univocality holding sway in the objective, real world. The status of objects in this space, and that of the phenomena occurring there, is double and must remain so until the child decides otherwise. The transitional object belongs to the Ego segment and to the non-Ego segment. Weening consists of transposing the object from the originary sphere into the sphere of reality, where its status changes from transitional object to real object. The parent and the child, together, invent the moment when the thing loses its double status, in order to become an object that exists. Existence, as Winnicott has shown, is the property acquired by the object after surviving a deadly attack. The object which exists is the one that survived the attack. The comfort blanket loses its irreplaceable object status, acquiring an objective common name and the status of an exchangeable object: it becomes a piece of cloth. The scientific object is born when originary duplicity—the Ego *and* non-Ego of the transitional object—is abolished. This same object is transferred from a sphere governed by a paradoxical system, a sphere we call originary, to a sphere governed by the principle of non-contradiction; that is, where an object cannot have two contradictory properties such as internal and external, Ego and non-Ego.

In the feeding relation, the maternal function safeguards the ambiguity of the status of objects and phenomena when it is still undetermined. A mother capable of the "primary maternal preoccupation", which Winnicott likened to a form of madness, ensures that an object can be at once good and bad, internal and external, objective and subjective. This potential space where phenomena and objects have a paradoxical status cannot be questioned or objectified without being destroyed. When relegation to the sphere of the real is untimely (the object loses its dichotomy), the child is unable to turn back on his parent and object to the separation to which the latter wishes him to submit. This ability to turn back on the parent relies on the parent's aptitude to remain in the role of adversary; an adversary who does not impose separation, but lets it be wrested away from him.

Winnicott's proposal of a potential space moves psychoanalytic theory into the sphere of monistic thought. Initially, outside and inside are one, they are not distinct; neither are Ego and non-Ego, good and bad and, we might add, imaginary and real. In this axiomatic perspective, the child is seen as having to set the limit between outside and inside in order to take ownership of it. When the right conditions are provided, he is able to invent the reality of objects. In this manner, Winnicott dispels the confusion created by Freud between the conditions of sense and sense, between "being" and "self".[2] In my book *From Freud to Kafka*,[3] I called the "being" the bedrock of the Ego—a paradoxical agency, open and closed, marked with the seal of primal repression. On this foundation, Sigmund Freud's metapsychology is pertinent, and the events of the world can acquire meaning. But if, as I am proposing, all the forms of psychopathology are related to a failure of primal repression, then the axiomatic edifice of psychoanalysis deserves to be established on foundations better able to take into account the phenomena occurring close to the origin. In other words, we are elaborating a change paradigm for psychoanalysis. From this perspective, the first element of the system to modify is the fundamental concept of instinct. This is so because when Freud introduced the concept—a self-referential concept involving the value of the limit—he assumed that the child could set a limit between inside and outside on his own; that this ability was given at birth. The concept of "instinct" implies discontinuity, present from the origin, when Freud considers the infant capable of distinguishing between the interior of his body and the outside world, judging by his ability to avoid or cope with stimuli. In his text "Instincts and Their Vicissitudes", Freud suggests that the "perceptual substance of the living organism will thus have found in the efficiency of its muscular activity a basis for distinguishing between an 'outside' and an 'inside'." But at the start of his essay Freud had warned the reader that:

> [the] ideas—which will later become the basic concepts of the science— [...] at first necessarily possess some degree of indefiniteness [...]. So long as we come to an understanding about their meaning by making repeated references to the material of observation from which they appear to have been derived, but upon which, in fact, they have been imposed. Thus, strictly speaking, they are in the nature of conventions [...]. It is only after more thorough investigation of the field of observation that we are able to formulate its basic scientific concepts with increased precision, and progressively so to modify them that they become serviceable and consistent over a wide area.[4]

Oedipus pays the price of sacrificing his sight for the major transgression he commits when he speaks to the sphinx instead of killing it. In Sophocles's tragedy, the Sphinx disappears. According to Jean-Joseph Goux, [5] this disappearance signifies the evacuation of the mysterious, of the religious, of the non-scientific. Oedipus is seen as founding science by eliminating the time interval in which contrary elements coexist. In this scene, under the reign of "all or nothing", the Enlightenment and Science emerge, but the powers of Darkness have disappeared, contrary to the comfort blanket, which subsists as a piece of cloth. The good–bad duality has been destroyed. The blind spot, a mirror in which the "I" can conceive of the Ego—this spot where thinking is suspended, becomes omnipresent, and everything can be explained. Oedipus's hubris culminates in his answer to the riddle of the sphinx, when speaking could in no way be suitable. If he gave the right answer, the Sphinx would disappear from sight; if the answer was wrong, the monster would kill the visitor. Oedipus's answer is an affront to the unrepresentable. Impious Oedipus abolishes the discontinuity that the rite commemorates. When he answers the Sphinx, when he thinks instead of acting, he consents to doing away with the origins. He then has, in Hölderlin's words, "one eye too many". He invites partisans of the Enlightenment to have faith in a belief confirmed by their experience: that Man can avoid acting and can answer once and for all the questions: "What is Man?"

The hubris of modern man is ushered in by a mythical hero, and is renewed by the Christian God. Oedipus, with his scientific mind, paid the price for everyone. As for Christ, according to Paul he is an embodied god who redeemed all men through his sacrifice. The price paid, by a tyrant or a divine being, should have freed humanity of the debt incurred at the origin. What debt? That owed for receiving the good–bad, the living-and-dying, the questions "Is it good? Is it bad?" Thanks to Oedipus, the loss of one's mind was no longer required; it was possible to keep one's head. For followers of Christ, indecision was prohibited. The true God, dead and resurrected, appeared in all his truth, and in the name of this alleged truth it was possible to enslave, to convert, to hunt down and to kill the "others". The uncertainty associated with the revealed texts was erased, and the renewal and enrichment of the interpretational in each successive generation—which is the foundation of the Jewish tradition—was no longer advocated or encouraged, but rather condemned, since the meaning was established once and for all, and an answer had finally been brought to the Question. Hence, the origins were no longer to be studied. At last, time could move more quickly and progress could take off decisively without bothering with the ritual celebration of the irrepresentable—a celebration requiring recourse to a great variety of means.

This definite inclusion of discontinuity into the conceptualisation of instincts had major consequences on clinical practice. The first was that it encouraged the belief that everything can be explained, and that it is always possible to work back from the effect to the cause, and to think that a causal curb can be derived for every phenomenon. Freud, who defended the notion of discontinuity Jung and Fliess disagreed with, included it in his fundamental concept—the instinct—and by effecting this arbitrary inclusion he in fact excluded discontinuity from any inquiry. He removed it from any possibility of modification, since it is given at the origin.

Finally, the concept of instinct stresses the intrapsychic and encourages the omission of the interpsychic. This led to attributing borderline pathology to archaic instincts, instead of conceiving of it as the effect of an inadequate holding environment early in life. Winnicott, with the concepts of holding and handling, and Lacan, with the notions of the symbolic and the imaginary, have given us crucial elements Freud had not identified as distinctive, but had associated with repression.

Once discontinuity was sealed in the foundations of Freud's theory, buried in the definition of *Grundbegriff*—the fundamental concept—it could claim to organise clinical practice. But the practice could not be therapeutic as long as it remained marked by a system of thought which assumed it had resolved the question of the separation of parent and child, and did not take into account intersubjectivity or the "properties" remaining indivisible between the parent and the child.

An invitation to renunciation was one of the clinical consequences of this tautological argument which grants the child, from the origin, the ability to construct for himself a closed and open originary realm, and which considers the infant a sphere where Ego instincts, guardians of life, compete with the internal seducer—the sexual instinct—for the preeminence the latter claims. A psychoanalyst subscribing to this way of thinking would forgo analysing, urging the patient to attribute his suffering to failed repression of incestuous and murderous instincts, after convincing him of their existence. Not only is the patient invited to consider the problem solved, but also to relegate it to the closed sphere of a self-produced instinctual apparatus.

A second important consequence is that a theory which considers solved, once and for all, the question of the limit between inside and outside leaves out of its jurisdiction—excluded from its purview—all those for whom this limit is problematic. This pushes psychosis outside the realm of its concerns, and not only psychosis as represented by the madman, but also by the psychotic nucleus present in all of us.

A consequence of this foregone conclusion was still apparent recently in discourses sanctioning certain groups claiming to be the guardians of orthodoxy. In order to maintain an ideal image of Freud and the literal respect of his teaching, harbingers in these groups were reporting that in contemporary psychopathology the types of problems encountered are different than those observed by Freud. In fact, these observers asserted to one and all that they rarely, if ever, saw cases of hysteria like Dora's or Emma's, and that most of the cases they saw involved narcissistic pathology or borderline disorders.

Another way of describing this is to say that Freud's initial discourse suffered from a pathology of continuity, that is, that repression of the ordinary which made possible the inclusion of the limit, blending the normal with the pathological in a frenzied need to explain it, and was the childhood illness of psychoanalysis, in its different forms. The fact that today analysts observe so many cases revealing borderline pathology can be attributed to researchers like Balint, Winnicott, Lacan, Abraham, Searles and a few others, who have changed the way we view our clinical work.

For today's practice to be coherent with the theory, we had to recognise that the importance of instinctual duality today is, above all, epistemological.

Instinctual monism as Freud originally perceived it, only to renounce it for the sake of "good sense" in 1919, is the theoretical revolution he left it up to his successors to make.

Notes

1 Rilke, R. M., *Duino Elegies*, Corn, A. (Trans.), New York, W. W. Norton, 2021.
2 At the end of his chapter "Creativity and Its Origins", in *Playing and Reality* (Routledge, 2005), Winnicott wrote: "After being, doing and being done to. But first, being".
3 Réfabert, P., *From Freud to Kafka*, London, Karnac Books, 2014.
4 Freud, S. (1915). *Instincts and Their Vicissitudes*, S.E.14, London: Hogarth.
5 Goux, J.-J., *Oedipus, Philospher*, Porter, C. (Trans.), Redwood City, CA, Stanford University Press, 1994.

2

A Transitional Psychic Matrix
A Proposal for Reflecting on Splitting and Fetishism

In 1938, a year before his death, Freud proposed the description—in truth, a sketch, because the article remained unfinished—of a defence mechanism. In it, he asks himself if his proposition is not "something entirely new and puzzling".[1] Indeed, he is saying that when an event causes horrible fright, the Ego finds a cunning (*kniffig*) solution to the problem—at the cost of an irreversible rift, it satisfies both competing parties: the instinctual demand and reality. This is how Freud describes a little boy's desire to masturbate, and the threat of castration coming from his governess. The conflict is resolved thanks to the splitting, and each of the two forces in conflict receives its share. Freud has just created a terrible problem for psychoanalysts. He has, in fact, presented them with a challenge. Indeed, at a time when the dramatisation of childhood conflicts, which exert great influence, constitutes the wellspring of psychoanalysis, Freud proposes a hypothesis in which the conflict is hidden in the symptom. Until then, psychoanalysis saw its reflection in tragedy; particularly in *Oedipus Rex*. Tragedy was its medium, a place where two forces fight over the destiny of a hero who must deal with them in order to enjoy a "difficult freedom". Splitting is radically opposed to repression, which distorts and hides the traces of a drama that can always be remembered. In the case of splitting, the event cannot be remembered and, above all, the two opposing forces can coexist peacefully. We have left the realm of the tragic for another type of theatre. This was a challenge to Freud's own thought, since the theory was based on mechanisms foreign to the split Ego. The metapsychology and the theory of the technique had been elaborated for repression, not for splitting. How was it going to be possible to find the source of psychic tension apparently hidden in the symptom, and which, in paranoia, is projected outward?

For 50 years, psychoanalysts have been trying to carry out the work that Freud kept taking up, abandoning and reworking again, in order to free psychoanalytic theory from the rigid philosophical framework of associationist theory in which a self-sustaining psychic monad enters into a relation with another monad. Many authors (Hermann, Ferenczi, Balint, Fairbairn, Abraham, Winnicott, Searles, Pankow and Lacan, among others) strove to integrate the other, earlier and more radically, into the conception of the genesis of the Ego. All of them contributed to this. The present work follows in their footsteps.

DOI: 10.4324/9781003435730-3

The Loss of Tutelary Agencies

The Lakotas, one of the North American Indian nations, say that a child is brought to his parents by a tutelary animal. If the parents don't provide the child with appropriate care, this animal will take him back. In my view, the threat of mutilation used by the governess to stop the masturbation of this "little boy between three and four years old" is part of the mistreatments that could cause the tutelary animal to take back the child; entirely or in part. A part of the child's ego would leave the human world, while the other would remain there. When this little boy rubbed his penis to reduce a feeling of distress, keeping himself awake by this excitement before starting to sway back and forth rhythmically, the governess's reaction was more than a threat of castration. If we imagine that, when the threat was made, the little boy had just discovered masturbation as a way of maintaining psychic integrity in the isolation in which this governess left him, then this child was in a situation where, to maintain a flow of stimulation that enables contact with the world, he could only have recourse to his body. If, at this time, when the body replaces the rest of the world, the governess proffers her threat, she incites him to give up a means of psychic survival. The child who has just discovered the dam of masturbation against the cessation of all sensory stimulation—that is, a line of defence to maintain a minimal link with the universe—sees this dam attacked by the governess.

In this borderline state, the child "between three and four years old" is in a situation where the threat can be believed, especially if aided by the tone of voice. The child's Ego splits when he must deal with an adult who pretends to be the protector of his body and soul, while at the same time denying him a means of survival in a moment of crisis.

Philoctetes' Betrayal

Betrayal held in suspense is the theme of Sophocles' tragedy in which Philoctetes is tricked by his own people, and then threatened with betrayal. The key dramatic device employed is the suspense in which spectator is held: will the betrayal take place or not? Tension is at its height when Neoptolemus is sent by the sons of Atreus to convince Philoctetes to join the army assembled before Troy. Neoptolemus is torn between his promise to Ulysses and his loyalty to Philoctetes, whose trust he has just gained and who has given him his magical bow. This double loyalty and this threat of betrayal make the play a tragedy. In the last scene, Heracles, who protects Philoctetes and gave him the magical bow, intercedes to encourage the hero to forego revenge and join the army.

Writing a play on the theme of betrayal carried through is a challenge. Our hypothesis is that betrayal does not take place, because if there was to be betrayal by the tutelary agency, it would be instantly erased. Here, betrayal would be suspended otherwise than in a tragedy: if its occurrence would cause psychic death, it would be abolished. Forgetting this betrayal is the price the individual pays to save his life and keep a place in the community.

If we were to write a "new Philoctetes" where the betrayal was carried out, we would not know how to classify it. We would not call it a tragedy, for this genre supposes a conflict between two forces which fight over a destiny. No, we would have to include it in the theatre of the absurd. In this new play, Heracles, the god who protects Philoctetes and gives him the magical bow and the arrows that never miss their mark, would come in at the start of the play. He would discourage Philoctetes from using his bow. This intervention would obviously seem absurd, since a god could not betray his word, showing himself to be both divine and diabolical; a god could not deceive. And yet, the unthinkable would take place. For instance, Heracles would tell Neoptolemus: "Keep this bow, go ahead. What difference does it make if it is he or you who has it?" Or he would say to Philoctetes: "After all, I lent you this bow, I didn't give it to you. And even if I had given it to you, you haven't shown much gratitude", or any other words bringing to mind the Jewish tale of the kettle, told by Freud at the end of Chapter 2 of *The Interpretation of Dreams*. But these words which would disavow the original gift would not be heard by Philoctetes, nor be the spectators (we would have to invent an appropriate theatrical device). Philoctetes would be astonished and Heracles's words would be forgotten, falling into the split that would instantly occur.

Philoctetes would keep his external appearance, but from then on he would be another, founded on a split into which the value of the bow has sunk and been swallowed up. The bow would exist, Philoctetes would speak of it, but he would no longer claim it, for he would have forgotten its value. At the same time, the Philoctetes he was before, the one driven by righteous anger, would lose his memory. Philoctetes would be deprived of his anger. He would be told that long ago he had violent fits of anger and that one day they suddenly stopped. Now, Philoctetes would be haunted by the fear that a breakdown which he did not experience could recur. The shipwreck has been engulfed by the split and the split is his new foundation. This division replaces his memory of the event. The unbearable produces a change in his Ego, modifying the dynamic organisation of space.

Since the catastrophe, Philoctetes has become docile and well-mannered, but as tyrannical as a morning glory on its support because he expects Heracles to dispense him of any risk of breakdown. Philoctetes has become Heracles's obedient and diligent slave. He is also understanding: he acknowledges his father's changeable character, but he can comprehend and justify it. As for Heracles, he is able to talk to his son about the childhood traumas that caused him to be such an inadequate father. Philoctetes cannot ignore these explanations. His anger is extinguished, and his ability to recognise the seductive, intrusive character of certain words is abolished. His tutor speaks of the shame he brought upon himself by failing in his function and taking back the bow. He even explains in what way this act is a repetition of what happened to Philoctetes in his childhood, and Philoctetes understands him. But while he understands him, he experiences bizarre sensations: he feels a draught blowing between his trunk and his limbs; his head is empty and he has the impression that his back is hollow. This is so unbearable that he is surprised he has not collapsed, but it never crosses his mind that there could be a relation between this sensation and what Heracles is saying, because his relationship with his tutor is considered indestructible. They are inseparable and cannot do without each other. He is the son, confidant and companion of the one he calls his best friend. He knows everything about Heracles's childhood, as well as about his loves. Heracles wants Philoctetes to know everything about him, and he considers nothing too intimate—be it the physiology of his tastes or that of his loves—to be included. Heracles can be imagined to say: "Friends like us, companions of misfortune, intelligent as we are, can hear everything, tell each other everything and understand everything".

Heracles would not stop conducting the trial of the father he was to his son. He would play the role of prosecutor, accusing himself of robbing his son, would be distressed, and would regret taking back the bow he gave him... Then Heracles would become his own defence lawyer and expose to Philoctetes all the suffering he himself endured as a child. But he would be very punctilious, especially in one regard: he would not tolerate Philoctetes questioning his qualities as a father. He would accuse himself, but his "light vessel cannot bear the slightest wind of accusation", especially from his son, who has had the incredibly good fortune to have had such an intelligent and liberal father. Heracles is intent on conducting his trial himself, and he remains intransigent on one point: he did not give Philoctetes the bow, he only lent it to him. Yes, he is as intransigent as Bluebeard was about using the closet.

This is the portrait we could make of this "modern Philoctetes", dispossessed of the bow Heracles gave him. No, Heracles remembers that he did not give him the bow, but only lent it to him.

By Way of Introduction to Ego Formation:
A Transitional Psychic Matrix

In order to devise his psychic apparatus—the foundation of his entire edifice—Freud presumes there is no problem left unsolved. He endows the Ego with a well-designed nucleus, with protective barriers and effective skills. Thus suitably equipped, and prior to any learning, the Ego is able to avoid being led down the alluring path of hallucinatory regression by the object of desire. Presumably, this well-designed nucleus can resist from the start the temptation of the sirens creating the hallucinatory object of desire. When he embarked on his research, Freud presumed that, from birth, the Ego has a "primary tendency to discharge tension", counteracted by a primary defence function which saves it from psychicdeath. These are some of the axioms of which the founder availed himself in order to create his field of research. A founding paradox is apparent in this aporetic tension Freud ascribed to the Ego from the start. This set of elements on which he founded his research, this unproblematic Ego with its presumed tendency to discharge and to hold back at the same time, constituted the cornerstone of his edifice. But this foundation was also what prevented him from integrating in his construction a discovery like splitting, because the Ego could not be equipped in the manner he described unless it was so from the beginning.

Since then, many authors, particularly in the Anglo-Saxon world—like Bion or Winnicott—have attempted to explore this axiomatic entity, the "well-designed Ego", and have proposed an alternative, making it possible to include clinical phenomena in the psychoanalytic field (such as splitting, borderline states or psychosis) that this axiomatic position excludes. Bion speaks of the mother's "ability to dream". Winnicott speaks of a "primary maternal preoccupation" enabling the mother to put herself in the place of a newborn to experience his needs.

Following in their footsteps, I suggest the existence of a psychic agency governing ego formation, and shared by the mother and the infant. This agency is the "place" where the mother imagines the child she expects, and where this child adjusts to her. This agency is both internal and external. The mother encounters the child in reality after having glimpsed him in the mirror of her dream. The child is hers because she recognises him as the child in her psychic matrix.

Not only is the real child recognised thanks to this psychic agency, but the mother adapts her languages—her words, her facial expressions, her gestures and her body rhythms—to this matrix. The child in the maternal matrix foreshadows the needs of the real child to whom the mother adapts. A real child has no needs: Man, immersed in language, has lost the codes available to animals, and it is the imagined child, the human double of the real child, who bestows the needs that will be his. The real child is introduced to the human sphere, to the semiotic universe of the needs of a son of Man, through the mirror used by the mother to fine-tune her exchanges with him. The "good-enough mother" addresses her child through this agency I propose to call "transitional psychic matrix".

As for the real child, endowed with this agency by his mother, he will be able to help her, at the right moment, to establish a harmonious relation between them after some adjustment. Thanks to this transitional psychic matrix, he too will be able to reestablish a harmonious exchange after an interruption. The real child will participate in the process through which his mother becomes a mother; he will aid her efforts to adjust to him. By doing so, he will participate fully in playing the musical score performed by the trio made up of the imagined child, his mother and himself. It goes without saying that this successful concertation will contribute greatly to the development of his self-confidence and his self-esteem right from the start. This can happen because the child has two points of reference: the transitional matrix and the real mother. Because the mother adjusts to this matrix and to the real child, the latter enters a human world where his mother can both recognise him and separate from him.

We shall have to define as best we can the relation between this agency and Freud's biological foundation. For the moment, suffice it to say that music comes closest to describing this relation. Music, a semiotic space without a signified where there is only spacing and note values, with no signified ever assigned to one of these elements, seems to be the semiotic domain most suited for illustrating this relation. It seems that the exchanges between cells, and between the cell and its milieu, take place at a certain rhythm (exchange of nutrients, of heat, etc.), and we can suppose that the psychic matrix is formed from the harmonic inscriptions of these rhythms. The origin of this agency, the transitional psychic matrix allowing the mother to be part of her child and the child to communicate with her, seems to be an amodal sensory matrix.

In summary, this transitional agency does not belong to the mother or to the infant, but to both of them. It is formed from an amodal sensory matrix set to the harmonics of rhythms compatible with life. Through its intercession, this agency, the guardian of psychic life, allows the child to be part of the mother, and the mother to be part of the child. When it exists, it is unfailing and indestructible: it provides the structure in which to resolve oppositions and contradictions that are part of the human condition and require leaps from one sphere of reflection to another. It is the guardian of discontinuity, of the possibility of passage. The function of this agency changes as the individual advances in age, but it never ceases; its breakdown always engenders harmful effects. I believe that keeping this agency in mind when considering ego formation is essential because this agency establishes self-esteem on a relational foundation, and even more importantly, it also establishes the possibility of self-esteem and of love of the other in oneself, that is, of transference and social relation. In short, this agency makes it possible to integrate clinical phenomena into the psychoanalytic sphere—phenomena which had been excluded or integrated clumsily.

Failure of This Agency: Its Replacement with a Fetish

A breakdown of this agency causes a pathological split in the Ego. When the mother does not see a child in this mirror, when the mirror is deserted or broken, the child is subjected to disorganised rhythms. For a child to gain access to psychic life, the elaboration of a psychic matrix must have been attempted. A child not recognised in the womb, who is not provided with rhythms compatible with life, might not be born, unless these conditions become the very early origins of a form of autism.

The Weight of the World

The unthinkable brought about by Heracles' disavowal in the fictional "new Philoctetes" consists of the disappearance of this mirror; the unexpected failure of this agency. When Heracles suddenly turns against his protégé, he not only destroys his trust, but mercilessly betrays their unbreakable bond and, at the same time, does not see, or pretends not to see, that this bond is Philoctetes' reason for living. In 1927, Freud spoke of disavowal in "Fetishism", [2] and the term seems well-chosen. The child responds to the breaking of an unbreakable tie by the disavowal of the relation between a perception and reality.

This unthinkable event did not take place because it is unthinkable for a parent to abandon his child at a critical moment for his bodily–psychic survival. Yet this is what happened, although, at the same time, it could not take place. The world, the *cosmos*, is a sphere governed by a certain order (the meaning of *cosmos*), which excludes this unthinkable possibility. "What happened" has no place in this world, and the child, who must remain in it at all costs, disavows the unthinkable that contradicts its order. This disavowal can be lifted after living through an end-of-the-world experience, hitherto warded off by the splitting.

The Fetish, Substitute for the Transitional Matrix

Sometimes, a child is forced to become the only guardian watching over his psychic life. The one in charge of this function has dropped the mirror he held up to him for a time. Since then, the other has lost his claim to participate in the maintenance of the child's psychic life. From then on, a concrete, visible substitute (the fetish) carries out this function, replacing the transitional matrix that was neither altogether him nor altogether the other, but shared and infallible, available to him for a time but forgotten now. A fetish is not a substitute for something lacking—supposedly a part of a woman's body—but a substitute for the transitional matrix. The fetish is the concrete substitute for a shared agency which takes up residence in a thing (an object, a practice, etc.). From then on, this substitute becomes the reassuring place, the only place worthy of complete trust. In this place, the individual will be able to go all the way to the limit, experience an orgasm without the risk of going mad. The orgasm, a striking illustration of human flexibility, of the ability to cross a border between two states—there and back—will henceforth be determined by this presence. A non-human entity will be the guardian of the passage.

Notes

1 Freud, S. (1938). *Splitting of the Ego in the Process of Defence*, S.E. 23, London: Hogarth, p. 275.
2 Freud, S., *Fetishism*, S.E. 21, London: Hogarth.

3

Maternal Donation and the Phallus

Consequences of a Construction

In psychoanalytic literature, fetishism holds a very particular place since, among the many psychoanalysts who keep trying to describe it and theories it, none—as far as I know—has ever had a fetishist come to him asking for therapy. Freud is no exception, although he does not say so explicitly. When he decided to "introduce an individual case history" in his "schematic disquisition",[1] he was speaking of a little boy faced with intolerable danger—the threat of castration made by a nursemaid—but he did not report on the symptoms of his adult patient, other than to say that as a child he had an intense fear of his father, which took the form of "a fear of being eaten by his father".[2]

I have no more clinical experience in this field than my colleagues, but I think that Freud's elaboration of fetishism—taken up again and validated by Lacan—signals a cessation of thinking, the stasis of psychoanalytic thinking. This concept remained based on the premises Freud developed in 1900, and did not take into account the theoretical step forward Ferenczi presented in 1929 at the Oxford Congress. Ferenczi's notion of the psyche–soma split in response to psychic trauma lays the foundation for the reshaping of the theory, and consequently of the practice.

The experience to which Freud attributed the origin of fetishism in the 1938 text entitled "Splitting of the Ego in the Process of Defence" can be summarised as follows: terrorised by the threat of castration, when the little boy glimpses the female genitals, he disavows reality to satisfy the demand (*Anspruch*) of libidinal instincts—and accepts it at the same time—to register an objection (*Einspruch*) to the same reality. Before seeing/not seeing the female genitals, the child elevates the last object he saw—a shoe, a garter—to the status of a "memorial". "The horror of castration has set up a memorial to itself in the creation of this substitute",[3] as Freud wrote in "Fetishism" in 1927. The fetish, this object entrusted with enabling sexual enjoyment, testifies to the inevitable ambivalence of an object symbolising both the presence and absence of a penis possessed by a woman, as well as the terror that produced this freeze-frame. The terror is forgotten, while the fetish—the memorial—remains as the sign of triumph (*das Zeichen des triumphes*) over the terror.

As for conceptualising the fetish, Lacan, like Freud, sees it as a substitute for the penis the mother is lacking, and they both proclaim it once again to be the fetishist's

DOI: 10.4324/9781003435730-4

object of desire. The subject then has an object which is "all the more perfectly sa-
tisfying for its being inanimate and devoid of any subjective, intersubjective, even
trans-subjective properties".[4] Here, Lacan gets carried away—as he is sometimes
wont to do—by his enthusiasm and his pleasure in provoking the proponents of the
"object relation". In the process, he can poke fun at the fetishist, who "will have
the peace of mind that it [the object] will not cause any disappointment. When the
subject loves a slipper, [he] truly has the object of his desires within reach".[5]

This way of looking at things is related to Lacan's idea of the founding trauma,
the first trauma suffered by the child expected to satisfy the mother's penis envy.
Caught in the grip of this trauma, the child rejects the one he is called upon to be
by maternal desire, a desire requiring him to be what he is not, in short, not to be or
to be a non-being. This initial expulsion (*Austossung*), when it does not produce a
fetish, creates the Real, a Real given the value -φ. The child, and later the adult, will
strive to "love" his fetish, or will wear himself out deciphering this Real, the fetish
or the Real representing the part of himself excluded *ab initio*.[6]

If Freud, and later Lacan, had heard the proposition made by Ferenczi at the Oxford Congress, they could have conceived of the idea that the fetish, the inanimate
object, could be a substitute for the child himself—the child who remained inanimate after a terrifying event which occurred without taking place, that is, without
finding a psychic place in which to be inscribed. In that case, the fetish would not
be, as Freud and Lacan think, a metonymic representation of the mother's genitals;
nor would it be an image that fell under the gaze of the terrified child. No, the fetish
would symbolise, at one and the same time, the murderous attack and the child left
for dead at that very instant, with no sign that anything had happened. Nothing appears to have happened because the child is immediately split in two: on one side a
living child left for dead, as if asleep; and on the other a second child who becomes
the uncompromising guardian of the first. The sign of triumph that Freud observes,
since he is an attentive clinician, testifies to the fact that a murder was committed.
The triumph is the sign of the attack and testifies to a manic episode *a minima* in a
child who survived attempted murder and is striving to act as if it never happened.

The "memorial" (*Denkmal*) that the fetish in fact is, is the sign of soul murder
perpetrated upon the child. The fetish is a substitute for his soul, left for dead, inanimate, as if in a deep coma. Gérard Pommier asserts that: "the real is somebody!",
and this someone is nothing other than "the part of oneself one has rejected". Pommier sees the fetish as "the part of the infant identified with the penis that the
mother is deemed to be lacking".[7] The *subject*, who underwent the founding sexual
trauma—the impossible identification demanded of him ("the real is the impossible") with a maternal phallus that is a void—devotes himself to the exploration of
the Real or... invents a fetish.

Following Freud's example, Lacan and Pommier suppose the child to be endowed with the ability to oppose non-being, the -φ that the maternal *Penisneid*
requires him to be. They believe that the child is naturally equipped to say "no" to
the siren calling to him to satisfy her *Penisneid*, her "penis envy". They presume
the newborn child capable of a primal "yes", a *Bejahung* bearing the trace of the

division of the subject, and constituting the irrefutable sign that the child has chosen life. But they do not explain why or how the child would choose to say "yes"
rather than opt for primary pleasure, that of *jouissance* leading to extinction, to
annihilation.

In my opinion, the newborn does not possess the ability to oppose non-being.
I think it essential to point out that the *Bejahung*, the consent to life, the "yes" to
life, is only effective if it is indissociably tied to an objection to death, a "no" to
becoming One. This donation of an objection to death, the gift of the trace of death,
is, in my view, the primordial counter-investment Freud sees as the mechanism of
primary repression.

When a woman possesses "her own death", as Rilke says, she invites the child to
join the "unavowable community"[8] which creates rituals to celebrate the adversary
that death represents for all speaking beings. The mother becomes the guardian
of life by taking death upon herself, and thus becoming the child's adversary. As
his *ad-versary*, she faces him, *ad-versum*, turned towards him constantly, even in
sleep. Thus, she forces the child to turn away from the easiest, the shortest path, that
of total satisfaction, of that orgastic discharge of all tension, the *jouissance*. This
counter-investment of the void creates the conditions needed for the validity and
viability of the *Bejahung*, of the "yes" to life.

When the mother objects to death in this manner, when she stands between the
child and the void, she transmits life against a backdrop of shadow, she forces the
child to respect himself—in the outmoded sense of "to respect" that refers to looking back. She forces him to look at this "form behind him", to see his image in her
eyes. By seeing the child on a backdrop of shadow, she gives him a limit, finitude.
She makes it possible for him to invent his own image, an image which represents
him, that is, symbolises his presence and his absence.[9] By doing this, she obstructs
a pure perception of the void; a pure perception that, as Rilke suggests in the Eighth
Elegy, will later astonish a lover who draws near.

In contrast, when the mother is not attentive to this counter-investment function and does not make an objection to death, or makes it inadequately because
she is busy hiding, denying or disavowing a *nameless thing*, an unpunished crime,
an unmourned loss, an unfelt pain; or because she is divided and consumed with
the task of covering over her split, the child must then grapple with the nameless
thing, instead of dealing with the trace of death, the trace of an event which albeit
unknowable, is recognised by the community and has rituals associated with it.
Above all, the child is required to compensate for the lack of maternal counter-
investment and the absence of an inscription of the trace of death in himself; to do
this, he will choose to sacrifice one of his functions or capacities, cancelling it out.

A mother, a parent, brings forth a child like God creates humankind, in his image
and likeness: "Let us make man in our image, in our likeness" (Genesis 1:26). If
we take into account the fact that the word "image", *tselem* in Hebrew, comes from
the same root as the word meaning shadow, darkness and idol; as well as the fact
that "resemblance" has the same root as the word meaning blood—synonymous
with life—we can say that the parent creates the child in the likeness of shadow

and light, in the image of death and life. The child is given life-and-death, inextricably linked. Humankind gives life on a backdrop of shadow, bestowing life and its representation, life limited by death. But when the child is created in a psychic matrix from which an event was cut out, this is no longer true. This omission can come about through a deliberate decision, like that made by Sutpen in Faulkner's *Absalom, Absalom!*[10]

Thomas Sutpen does not acknowledge the existence of his firstborn son, because he has "a single drop of black blood". His silence leads to incest between this son and his half-sister. This phenomenon can also be tied to the incorporation by the child of a parent's repressed representation, or can be due to nescience (in the third generation). This thing, that cannot be the object of any transmission, is to remain excluded from representation—its representation is prohibited—and can therefore never acquire—paradoxically—exteriority status.

Freud had the merit of opening the path of primal repression, even if he turned away from it almost at once; Lacan had the merit of reopening it by inventing the concept of subject ensuing from it: "The subject consists solely of the *Urverdrängung* [primal repression], the necessary collapse" of the first signifier, but "cannot be a substitute for it as such, since the representation of a signifier is a substitute for another signifier, not for a subject". Lacan asserts that the original signifier is the maternal phallus, - φ.

I would like to suggest that the phallus is not the original signifier, but the first (S1), which testifies to the disappearance of the primordial signifier (So), the trace of death. The action of the first metaphor confers the value of the primordial signifier—the trace of death—to the first signifier[11] - φ, which covers over, hides, sends into oblivion, the primordial signifier. This *dropping* away—illustrated by the Fall in Genesis—of the trace of death is the result of the primal repression.

While the choice of the phallus as primal signifier indicates that the child is considered equipped to turn away, alone, from the path shown by his primal desire, the choice of the trace of death takes into account the need for the active donation made by the *Nebenmensch*—although an animal can sometimes play this role. The primal repression creates the field of the narrative, of the fiction, of the space of the founding illusion of existence, an essential illusion born of the fading into oblivion of the original signifier.

To return to sexual trauma, in our opinion the little boy's reaction to seeing the female genitals, the way in which the evidence of the difference between the sexes is assimilated, how the child—boy or girl—withstands the violence of the symbolic, depends on the quality of the maternal donation, the objection the mother raised to the unlimited. This maternal donation is made at the very beginning of the child's existence, both in the womb and after birth, through a rhythmic alternation of incitations and pauses. This alternation of sensory incitations and pauses in which the child is immersed provides him with a foundation which constitutes the source of his libido and the indestructible core enabling him to sustain, without breaking down or splitting, the paradox of the difference between the sexes, and the difference between generations. Primal *ananke* is what is present when a living being supports, for and with the child, the primary paradoxical conditions of his existence.

When the sight of the female genitals is traumatic for the little boy, when accepting the difference between the sexes is problematic, it can be surmised that the child has suffered a psychic shock that expelled him from the space created by the primary paradoxical conditions that constituted his foundations until then. When the child is subjected to a murderous attack, to soul murder, he finds himself instantly displaced, inconspicuously, from the protected and exposed site that had been his. In the course of this attack, this soul murder, the trace of death initially given to him is taken away and the child must, *instantly*, to counteract the sudden destruction of the subject, perform a division—disunite to create at his own cost an artificial division: a split.

The maternal donation consists of "taking the bad into oneself". Freud writes: "What is bad, what is alien to the ego [...] are, to begin with, identical".[12] The mother relieves the child of his double who is doomed to die, thereby becoming his guardian to protect him from death. On the contrary, soul murder, or the mother's passionate desire to be as one with the child, makeshim an innocent child exposed to all the dangers that a tyrannical watchman, the other face of the same child—but split off—strives to confront, so as to become his own adversary.

This perspective requires further comment on the concept of the death drive. From my point of view, the death drive is no longer—as in Lacan's perspective interpreted by Pommier—the attraction exerted on the child by the mother's passion to satisfy her *Penisneid*, her "penis envy";[13] here, the child is no longer forced to resist identifying with - φ, with the missing phallus, to oppose on his own an attraction that would destroy him. No, the death drive in this new perspective is related to the mother's desire for *indifferentiation*, her desire to be as one. It is the expression of the mother's passionate desire to erase a discontinuity, a singularity; and it is the sign of the incorporation by the child of the insistence of a nameless thing prohibited from coming into existence.

When - φ replaces the trace of death, assuming the status of primary signifier, a big piece of clinical practice crumbles because conducting an analysis based solely on sexual difference is like the vista discovered at the summit by a mountain climber who has been brought there by helicopter. For him, the problem of the climb is solved in advance.

Notes

1 Freud, S. *Splitting of the Ego in the Process of Defense*, S.E. 23, London: Hogarth, p.276.
2 *Ibid*. p. 278.
3 Freud, S., *Fetishism*, S.E. 21, London: Hogarth, p. 154.
4 Lacan, J., *The Object Relation: The Seminar of Jacques Lacan, Book IV*, Miller, J.A. (ed.), Cambridge, Polity, 2022.
5 *Ibid*.
6 Lacan considers the second trauma related to the Oedipus complex. It occurs when the child encounters the father as a rival and has to kill him in fantasy to take his place in the mother's life and thereby escape her fate.

7 Pommier, G., *Qu'est-ce que le "Réel"?*, Toulouse, Érès, 2004, p.23.
8 Blanchot, M., *The Unavowable Community*, New York, Station Hill Press, 2006.
9 Representation is not a repeated presentation, but an intensive presentation where presence and absence are combined. See Jean-Luc Nancy, "Forbidden Representation", in *The Ground of the Image*, Fort, J. (Trans.), New York, Fordham University Press, 2005.
10 Faulkner, W., *Absalom, Absalom!*, New York, Modern Library, 1993.
11 Lacan has stated emphatically that it is to the degree to which the mother conveys, or not, the paternal metaphor, the extent to which she is inscribed and inscribes herself in the order of symbolic exchange, that she ensures primal repression and promotes, or does not, the emergence of a subject.
12 Freud, S., *Negation*, S.E. 19, London: Hogarth.
13 This way of thinking follows from the choice of the phallus as primary signifier.

4

Rhythmic Concertation and Its Disruptions

— Are you dead?
— Yes, said the hunter [...]. Many years ago [...] — I fell from a rock in the Black Forest
[...] as I was tracking a chamois. Since then I've been dead.
— But you're also alive, said the burgomaster.
— To a certain extent, said the hunter, to a certain extent I am also alive. My death ship
lost its way
— a wrong turn of the helm...

Franz Kafka, "The Hunter Gracchus" in Kafka: Selected Stories,
West Valley City, UT, Waking Lion Press, 2008.

The singularity that the child is given the possibility to acquire is related to the objection the mother raised when she expulsed the child. By this we do not mean the physiological expulsion of birth, but rather the effect of an inclination which impels her to forego her omnipotence, to hold death—discontinuity—in check, as Abraham did with Isaac on Mount Moriah. The good enough mother lets the child, at every age and stage of his development, advance on the crest, where he can bear the tension between life and death, between open and closed, between pleasure and jouissance, between infinite and finite, between yes and no. This inclination of the mother inspires her to let the child invent the breast she does not give him, but which he has to create. This gift becomes the foundation of a temperament seen as attributable to "chance" in a perspective tending to objectify.

The repression of the original paradox—life and death—appearing in the form of a gift "to create", is a paradoxical foundation constituting the foundation of the subject. The fold that the trace of death leaves in the subject provides him with an image of himself, making reflection possible. This image is the form taken by the interweaving of presence and absence. In my view, this fold is akin to the "shadow" referred to by Hugo von Hofmannsthal, and I propose to call "shadow" this fold resulting from originary repression. To have a shadow means to have a "bodily" memory of discontinuity; of the trace of death in your own person.

A man or a woman with no shadow would be someone with no link to the expulsion from the Garden of Eden. Universal discontinuity, the foundation of the

DOI: 10.4324/9781003435730-5

human community—the discontinuity usually integrated by taking the form of an objection—has lost its symbolic character in this case, and with it its universal nature. The private discontinuity that has come to replace it has no name, and therefore no existence. Here, the trace of death has been erased, replaced by the trace of an inaccessible thing which cannot be shared and, above all, cannot be found, and which precludes reflection, making it impossible to turn back on oneself, to see oneself.

A mother ousted from the community of those who have been marked by fundamental discontinuity, who bear the trace of death, expects her child to give her back her place in that community. A mother with no shadow may search for it ruefully and expect her child to give it to her, expect him to give her the shadow she does not know she lacks. At the same time, she lures him into the no-place she does not know that she inhabits. She acts as if she wants the child to swallow her, so that she may share his vital energy, but acts at the same time as if she wants to draw him into her no-place. In this contradictory dynamic, no harmony can be established between them. She only knows a system of *all or nothing*, and she maintains the child in servitude, or she wounds him. Alternatively, she lures him, seduces him and hurts him... only to tend to his wounds.

Such a mother, when she is not cold and indifferent—which is worse—has the painful feeling of being unable to establish harmonious relations with her child. She approaches him and would like to fill the invisible chasm that keeps him out of reach. This desire causes her to share her adult concerns with him, even turning him into a confidant. Tormented by the feeling that there is *nothing* between them, she tells him *everything* about her unhappiness, her distress, her childhood suffering, her loves.She tells him about her sex life and talks to him about her death. The voice that retorts to all this is that of a patient of mine, who is repeating the words of his father: "If you can't talk about this to your child, tell me, who can you talk to—isn't that right?" Such a parent counts on turning his child into an expert therapist, and asks him to understand him, to bring him to life.

In this *all or nothing* system, truth holds a special place. Its fate resembles that of all the attempts to establish a relation between the child and a mother alive "to a certain extent": they fail. Truth is a two-sided figure to which the parent ousted from his originary foundation, from his childhood, clings. He clings to it because from where he stands the truth looks like reality. But this objective reality, "realistic", is false when it hides the exclusion of the subjective, embodied part of the subject. A parent exiled from himself only has objectivity and principles to guide his actions. Cut off from his subjectivity whose trace he has lost, cut off from his shadow, he resorts to and appeals excessivelyto reason. The child is overwhelmed with revelations about the mother's intimate life, even about her future death, and the nature of her relations with the child's father. This complexity is fostered in the wild hope of filling the gap between them, but it only serves to widen it. It widens the gap while creating an immediate bond, a relation akin to incest.

This parent appeals to the child's reason to prevent him from exploring the hidden side of things, he stops him from losing his time and plays the role of an

Aristotelian philosopher or a Medieval theologian for whom time is only a degraded form of eternity. By doing this, he intends to dissuade Achilles from entering the race with the tortoise. What good is this race, since the enterprise is unrealistic? This parent cannot tolerate any paradox at all, and what he wants first and foremost is to prevent the child from understanding a temporality that includes discontinuity, the movement and exploration of the past. He has no access to what is not but exists nevertheless, and he thinks the story of the burning bush is nonsense. He only believes in one thing, just as Don Juan did: "I believe that two and two make four; four and four, eight".[1] Only the present interests him. As for play, this parent invites the child to play, but only educational games, not just play for *no reason*.

In the same spirit opposed to flights of fancy, the parent virtuously opposes all illusion arising in the potential space of play. Let us come back to the child whose parent sought and found in him the image of himself that no mirror reflected.

A mother with no shadow tries relentlessly to see herself in her child's gaze, to reassure herself of her own existence rather than step back and reflect the child's face. The child disappears at once, feels himself falling into a void or liquefying.[2] All his life, the threat of this experience will hang over him, and its aftershocks will come about unexpectedly in the form of a train that bursts into the parlour, or bell towers that start to dance. These aftershocks seem to be preceded by certain signs, or by events like the end of a love relationship or a friendship. Each time, they bring about the feeling that time has stopped its flow, that it has become a solidified mass of present. It is exceedingly painful to be unable to feel that time has limits. A person caught in this no-place, and who is also out of time, finds himself exiled from his own body and from the world. Blindly, in order to return to the world, he may throw himself headlong against his companion, or even into a wall. Sometimes he tries to "reconstruct" himself in a sexual orgy, or he drinks to the point of ethylic coma, only to be overwhelmed with shame afterwards.

The child lives in fear of being abandoned by such a parent. But his terror is like a hiding place, a veil protecting him from reality. For what he perceives as a threat of being abandoned has to do with his fear of losing the nominalistic mirage that makes his parent a "father" or a "mother". A parent who was divested of his shadow acts as if he was only tied to the child by the bonds that the latter weaves between the parent and himself. In this situation, the child is expected to ensure the existence and solidity of the tie between him and the parent, as well as that between the parent and him—but invisibly—while remaining in his "child place". The threat of abandonment he feels protects him from the reality of having always been left on his own. In such a configuration, separating from the parent is impossible.

The child's guilt also comes from feeling in his body the sensation of the "death" of his parent, or perhaps I should say "of the reality of the death of the parent". Such a sensation, felt before a parent who demands consideration, support and equanimity in the face of his intrusions, causes the child to formulate the inadmissible wish to see his parent dead. Only his body grants itself permission to physically push away this parent whose closeness sickens him. But he feels guilty about that too.

I believe that Franz Kafka, who sometimes saw bell towers dancing in the sky over Prague, knew the cost of having been the precocious therapist of such a parent. Many of his short stories, like *The Hunter Gracchus*, testify to this. This character, unlike Don Juan, knows that he is dead and when the burgomaster of the village where his boat enters the port asks him if he is dead—a dove had announced the hunter's arrival during the night—the hunter confirms it and adds, to answer the burgomaster's question, that he is also alive "to a certain extent". Since his death and the unfortunate wrong turn of the helm, the hunter travels on "through all the countries of the earth" on his ship, where "the basic mistake of [his] death grins at [him] in [his] cabin".[3]

Someone who was an early therapist of the living dead will have great difficulty separating from him and establishing with him a relation that acknowledges reality, the reality of a parent who is alive "to a certain extent". But this separation is always facilitated by the search undertaken with the analyst for the woman or the man—the living being—who colluded with the living dead and enabled him to come alive. In many cases, a domestic servant, a school mate, a grandparent or a brother played this role. Sometimes, an animal—a dog, a cat, a horse—was an essential ally. This is an important phase in the analysis: the search for and the discovery of the being who, most often secretly, was able to acquaint the child with the vital pleasure of rhythmic concertation, of polyphonic writing, of ethical living in a space of time where esthetics and ethics are indissociable.

I have had occasion to be particularly impressed with the description by an analysand of an uncontrollable emotion felt while she held a rabbit—*a doe*—a child left with her. This overwhelming emotion led us back to *Aline*. This patient had been adopted, as it were, almost from birth, by Aline, a servant who cared for her with warmth, attention and love. With Aline, there was room for tears, affection and even anger against the one who loved her. The little girl and Aline were engaged in a secret mother–child relationship. The family accepted the bond with this "stepmother", but knew little about it. The relation was tolerated without being recognised. The child slept in Aline's bed and later shared her room. They were inseparable, but the relation was never mentioned by the family, so that in her adolescence the young girl had forgotten the person to whom she owed her life, and only remembered her in analysis. This discovery conferred on the patient's childhood a completely new time and space dimensionality, contrasting with those that had consisted of humiliation, offenses and repeated soul murder. I must add that this patient was the only child in the family tacitly entrusted to this employee who, on her part, "adopted" her; this exception, I thought, explained the fact that she was also the only one among her siblings who had not suffered a psychotic break.

An analyst–patient couple unable to identify the person who truly gave life, in the sense of giving life *and* the trace of death—the person who adjusted to the child's vital rhythm to give him a time-space, an ethical existence and an aversion for any kind of servitude—such a couple would be condemned to wander aimlessly and endlessly replace one symptom with another.

Notes

1 Molière, *Don Juan*, Act III, sc. 1.
2 See the writings of Geneviève Haag, particularly "Le moicorporel entre dépression primaire et dépression mélancholique" (The Physical Ego Between Primary and Melancholic Depression), *Revue française de psychanalyse*, No. 68/4, 2004.
3 Kafka, F., "The Hunter Gracchus", in *Kafka: Selected Stories*, West Valley City, UT, Waking Lion Press, 2008.

5

On Expulsion

Isaac and Ahab

The story of the bounding of Isaac can be read as a reply to the original, founding paradoxical injunction: "Of every tree of the garden though mayest freely eat. But of the tree of knowledge thou shalt not eat, for in the day that thou eatest thereof thou shalt surely die". This well-known story is about Abraham's and Isaac's greatness of soul on the one hand, and about the miracle of a divine intervention which interrupted a cruel trial—whereby a father would have had to show his heroic submission to God, who had ordered him to sacrifice his beloved son. I propose that we read this story as a reply to the original paradoxical injunction; in this case, a father would be obeying the paradoxical injunction: "Lay him on the altar, take him down". Here, the resolution of this paradoxical injunction, of this aporia, takes the form of a ram sacrificed to God,[1] a ram substituted for the expected lamb—a few verses earlier, Isaac did in fact ask: "Father, where is the lamb?" The sacrifice of the ram symbolizes *both* the murder *and* forfeiting the murder. But whose murder? The traditional interpretation is that it is Isaac's murder. But I see another possible reading: the sacrifice of this adult animal can symbolise the fact that Abraham forfeits the right to survive his son. Here, a father accepts his own mortality, establishes the succession of the generations and embodies temporality. As for the son, he is marked with the trace of death passed on to him by the trial undergone by his father, and is thus inscribed in time. And time, as we have known since St. Augustine's discussion of its nature, is paradoxical.

Henceforth, Isaac relies on the support of a father who accepts the fact that his son will outlive him. Abraham, from this position where he supports human existence—that is, life implying death—offers support to his son and to Sarah, his wife. His son will laugh—it is his name, Itzchak. His wife laughs when she learns she is with child. The wife and the son laugh because the father has forfeited a perpetual present and the possibility of exerting limitless power. Each person in this constellation will build on the "forgotten" bottomless depth, which Freud considers to be the primal repression.

In some cases, the parent does not build on the bottomless depth. This task is left to the *infans*. Such a parent can only "hold up" by supporting himself on the *infans*, who lets the parent lean on him, against him, without letting go. But at what cost? At the cost of inventing some symptoms chosen from a whole range of possible

DOI: 10.4324/9781003435730-6

symptoms, often foregoing anger, which in Greek is *orguè*, the root of "orgasm". Sometimes, in adolescence or in adulthood, the child of such a parent will have a panic attack, and will feel as if it's the end of the world and he is losing his footing.

A figure opposed to that of Isaac, whose father assumes their mortality, is that of Ahab, Herman Melville's hero. Captain Ahab is in command of the Nantucket whaling vessel Pequod. Ahab has always hunted whales, first as a sailor, as a harpooner and then as the first mate, before becoming a captain. While he was first mate, he lost a leg when he attacked Moby Dick, the white whale. On the return voyage, Ahab was consumed with fever and suffered from delirium, so that he was bound, not like Isaac, but in a straight-jacket. Since then, he has had a peg leg. As for his name, it was given to him by his "crazy" mother, Melville tells the reader. Ahab[2] is the name of the worst king of Israel, who built a temple where his idols were to be worshipped, and who let his wife falsely accuse Naboth of blasphemy so that he could take possession of Naboth's vineyard. The prophet Elija had predicted that Ahab, as brave and fearless a soldier as he was a bad king, would die alone in his chariot, and the dogs would lick up his blood.

Melville portrays Ahab as a figure torn between his fierce hatred of the white whale and the fear with which this violent passion fills his soul:

> Ahab would burst from his state room, as though escaping from a bed that was on fire [...]. For, at such times, crazy Ahab, the scheming, [...] steadfast hunter of the white whale [...], was not the agent that so caused him to burst from [his cabin] in horror].[This] was the eternal [...] soul in him; and in sleep, being for the time dissociated from the characterizing mind, which at other times employed it [...], it spontaneously sought escape from the scorching contiguity of the frantic thing, of which, for the time, it was no longer an integral. [...] Nay [his one supreme purpose] could live and burn, while the common vitality to which it was conjoined, fled horror-stricken from the unbidden and unfathered birth.[3]

From this no-place where he is consumed with rage, Ahab sees that he is deemed to be mad. But he knows that in truth he is demoniac:

> They think me mad—Starbuck does, but I'm demoniac, I'm madness maddened. That wild madness that's only calm to comprehend itself! [...] I now prophesy that I will dismember my dismemberer.[4]
> ... all evil, to crazy Ahab, [was] visibly personified and made practically assailable in Moby Dick. He piled upon the whale's white hump the sum of all the general rage and hate felt by his whole race from Adam down.[5]

Indeed, Ahab's situation is comparable to that of Adam, had he been confined to Paradise for life—that is, to innocence, this no-place without any contradictions:

> Gifted with the high perception, I lack the low, enjoying power; damned, most subtly and most malignantly damned in the midst of Paradise![6]

It was an innocent mother, cut off from what happened to her, from the psychic anguish into which her soul was plunged, who confined Ahab to paradise. The submersion she suffered excluded the possibility that she could receive a paradoxical foundation and, since what happened—that which did not take place, did not find a psychic place—she was deprived of an existence combining life and death. She survived this psychic anguish, but in a state of innocence.

Banished from herself, as it were, she has survived a catastrophe all in one piece, with no access to the terror lurking in her body; she has nothing to do with it, has nothing to ask of anyone and has nothing to give. When her son was born, she came alive, not because of the love she felt for him, but because of her passionate desire to become one with him; this is how she loved him, by making him a transitional object one throws away after having first inhaled his scent greedily. Thus, she showered him with torrents of substitute Eros, yet mistreated him as well. This passionate impulse brought him into the world without expulsing him. The negation needed was not in her power to give.

This is how it comes about that Ahab is seized with rage at the threshold of the forgotten zero moment in time, the time when humans enter history. And this is why Ahab incites his crew to hunt before him what is not behind him, except from our perspective; to chase the betrayal of a promise—the promise of an expulsion. This non-event, the birth of Ahab, is *unheimlich*, as familiar and natural as it is strange and monstrous because there was no expulsion. This explains his frenzied attempt to expulse himself, to give himself the fold of existence.

Ahab is obsessed by the passionate desire to acquire a paradoxical foundation on which to build. He does not have a place in the history established by the social institutions governing dealings between men, justice, commerce and power. He takes care to respect them enough to avert suspicion and to subvert them, until his world reaches the point of no return, like an airplane at the moment of takeoff. Ahab is searching for the pure event. He is chasing after the signifier zero, which is acquired, fixed, forgotten, repressed at the origin, as it is for the sailors who make up the crew of the Pequod. Ahab is searching for a way to tie the bottomless depth to existence. He is seeking what everyone else has: forgetfulness, the time at the beginning which precedes history and can only be narrated in mythical form.

This is what fascinates the sailors, what makes Ahab the brother of false Messiahs. He is desperately seeking the paradoxical foundation that the men in his crew do not know they have. These men resemble the spoiled children of forgetfulness, because they had a parent who opposed the void, stood on the bottomless depth; they are the spoiled children of space and temporality, unaware of the support their mother gave them, thanks to good scansion, a correlate of facing her death.

This support is the symbol of the bottomless depth of the *Abgrund* the mother opposed by sensing its presence and choosing instead the emerging rhythmic form. This support which symbolises the fundamental aporetic unit—affirmation/negation, life/death, light/shadow, incitation/scansion—is Ahab's missing leg. This privation/amputation has made him a stranger among his fellow seamen, precluding

ties of camaraderie with the officers, and depriving him of the company of first
mates.

> He lived in the world, as the last of the grizzly bears lived in settled Missouri.
> And as when spring and summer had departed, that wild Logan of the woods,
> burying himself in the hollow of a tree, lived out the winter there, sucking his
> own paws; so, in his inclement, howling old age, Ahab's soul, shut up in the
> caved trunk of his body, there fed upon the sullen paws of its gloom![7]

Ahab's obstinacy has to do with the gloom of which he was deprived, but which
finds him, against his will, "in the caved trunk of his body, [feeding] upon the sullen paws of its gloom".[8] Deprived of a founding "no", of an originary negation, of
a clear rhythmic scansion, one of the elements forming the paradoxical foundation
of the being, he doesn't know how to find it.

Melville indicates Ahab's devotion to his mother's innocent soul through the
story of his hero's unfailing friendship for her stand-in, Pippin, "Pip" for short, an
"insignificant" Black cabin boy, slight and fearful, who is left stranded in the sea
during a whale hunt. Caught up in the rope holding the harpoon, left in the ocean,
he was rescued by the merest chance by the Pequod.

> ... from that hour [he] went about the deck an idiot; [...]. The sea had leeringly
> kept his finite body up, but drowned the infinite of his soul. Not drowned en-
> tirely, though.[9]

After this, Pip wandered on the deck like a simpleton, like an innocent soul. And
what was Ahab doing while he incited his men to rush forth and be shattered against
Moby Dick's massive head? He held Pip by the hand, speaking to him tenderly
while they strolled together on the deck. Pip is a substitute for himself and for the
mother who must have forgotten her psychic death, the moment when the vital tension, the difference in potential between life and death, had been reduced to nothing.

Starbuck, the Pequod's first mate, is another essential character in Ahab's world.
Unlike the other members of the crew, he knows where Ahab is leading them all,
but he can do nothing to avert the catastrophe.

Starbuck is introduced in the chapter where Ahab has brought the crew together
to convince them of the need to chase the white whale. To do this, he flatters his
own ego as well as that of the crew and each of its members, distributes great quan-
tities of grog, promises a gold doubloon to the first man who spots Moby Dick, and
holds out a lyrical challenge that enthralls his men. The whole crew is enthusiastic,
except Starbuck, who remains silent and long-faced. When questioned, Starbuck
bravely declares that he is there to earn a living, and that what he earns depends
on how much sperm oil he brings back to the market in Nantucket. And he adds
that he is not there to carry out his captain's vengeance.[10] But he soon has cause to
regret his daring, for Ahab launches into a rhetorical windstorm that sweeps over
the deck, until Starbuck pales and shivers. When Ahab adds in an aside: "Starbuck

now is mine; cannot oppose me now", the first mate murmurs, defeated: "God keep me!—keep us all!"[11]

Two chapters later, Starbuck is talking to himself, leaning against the mainmast:

My soul is more than matched; she's over-manned, and by a madman! […] I think I see his impious end; but feel that I must help him to it. Will I, nill I, the ineffable thing has tied me to him, tows me with a cable I have no knife to cut. […] Oh! I plainly see my miserable office, —to obey, rebelling; and worse yet, to hate with touch of pity![12]

It was as though Starbuck understood his mad forefathers, and loved them because he knew the *infans* in them, who could not speak, nor grow, and who sometimes, fleetingly, showed themselves in an expression, a surprising gesture, a quiver. So when he saw his captain near him, leaning over the side of the ship, and heard him say: "Oh, […] it is a mild, mild wind", and then go on to review his career, speak of his wife, whom he had made "a widow with her husband alive", and finally confess "the madness, the frenzy" with which he chased his prey, Starbuck's heart softened: "Oh, my Captain! my Captain! noble soul! grand old heart, after all! why should any one give chase to that hated fish! Away with me! let us fly these deadly waters! let us home! […] Let us away! — this instant let me alter the course!"[13]

But before he can finish his plea, turning pale with despair, Starbuck sees the captain avert his gaze and hears the blasphemous ravings Ahab utters, as he watches an albatross chase and kill a flying fish, concluding that God himself, who commanded this murder, is guilty of it. Dumbfounded, Starbuck makes no attempt to explain that Ahab confuses ethics with the laws of nature. Yet he remains clear-headed: "But shall this crazed old man be tamely suffered to drag a whole ship's company down to doom with him?"[14]

Despite his lucidity, Starbuck cannot act, even when he is holding the loaded rifle and talking to himself outside the door of the cabin where Ahab lies asleep. At that moment, he could turn the situation around, change fate—his own and that of the 30 crewmen—and prevent Ahab from carrying out the crime to which his "madness" leads him. But Starbuck is a good illustration of the son of a mad parent, a son who foregoes establishing a human order, who gives up living to preclude the possibility of causing his angry parent to collapse. Before giving up, Starbuck asked himself:

But is there no other way? no lawful way? — Make him a prisoner to be taken home? […] Say he were pinioned even, knotted all over with ropes and hawsers; chained down to ring-bolts on the cabin floor; he would be more hideous than a caged tiger, then. I could not endure the sight; could not possibly fly his howlings; all comfort, sleep itself, inestimable reason would leave me on the long intolerable voyage.[15]

Destruction is not the only outcome imaginable. In this spirit, I wrote an alternative to the end of the chapter. I wrote it thinking of the Ahabs who have come to see me, and still do, and seem to be expecting something of the analyst I am. In these circumstances I have often dreamt of embracing the innocent, raging baby, the living newborn the analysand does not know he carries inside him.

* * *

Starbuck puts down the rifle, goes up on deck and turns over command of the Pequod to Stubb, telling him to set course for Nantucket. He goes down again, opens the door of Ahab's cabin and throws himself on the sleeping man. He kisses him, holds him very tight and speaks to him softly.

Ahab, you are not the captain anymore, you are the infant you never were. If I have to, I will endure your wounded, enraged animal screams through the entire homeward voyage. No matter what, I will help the one inside you who has been trying to flee paradise, who struggled desperately to let himself out of it. For a long time I was intimidated by your integrity and strong determination. Yes, I was afraid of you for a long time, but today I will not put you in a straight-jacket like the commander of the ship did when your "torn body and gashed soul bled into one another" and made you "a raving lunatic" after Moby Dick tore off your leg.

No, today I hold you in my arms because I know that what you want to kill is whiteness itself, you want to kill innocence. I have you and I won't let go because I too will have to account for my actions. Remember that the Hebrew for "holding to account" is *pequod*, the name of your ship.

I love you, Ahab, and I refuse to see you punished—*pequod* again—for having desired to get revenge—*pequod* once more—by sacrificing your crew.

This demon you are chasing, Ahab, is the unbound to which you were condemned without a trial. The rage that made you howl in agony let you set a limit, somehow or other, and allay the bleeding of your soul. "I'm all aleak myself", you told me when you would not let me see the hold where the barrels of oil were leaking. But today, Ahab, I hold you in my arms and I will not let go.

During this cosmic battle which was to last for the duration of the return voyage, Starbuck continued to talk to himself, to keep up his courage:

I am holding you with all my might, scream as much as you want. You have been plundered by an innocent birth mother who did not bring you into the world, but bewitched you; she made you swallow this whiteness you abhor, this unredeemed filth. The one who claimed to be a mother captured you only to find refuge in you. Thanks to you, she could have a skin, no less. Disguised as pure innocence, she was a ravishing wolf. But wait, I am confused, I'm losing my head, it's just the opposite: she turned you into a ravishing wolf and became a lamb so you would swallow her.

You are a wolf, furious and enraged. Against whom? Against the whiteness. But be careful, it is inside you, not before you. The lookout you sent to the crow's nest in the mast will not see the lamb you chase in yourself, but rather the whale you told him to spot.

When the struggle had lasted a week, Starbuck, bruised and bitten, exhausted, heard—unless he imagined it—Ahab whisper: "Tighter! hold me tighter!"

Notes

1 According to one *Midrash*, Abraham is tested by God, who creates conditions leading him to imagine that he is being asked to sacrifice his son.
2 In Hebrew, Ahab sounds like the contraction of *ach*, brother, and *ab*, father. This makes him a distant relative of Oedipus, his sisters' brother and father.
3 Melville, H., *Moby Dick*, New York, Signet, 2013.
4 *Ibid.*
5 *Ibid.*
6 *Ibid.*
7 *Ibid.*
8 *Ibid.*
9 *Ibid.*
10 The Hebrew word for vengeance is *pequod*.
11 Melville, H., *Moby Dick*, op. cit.
12 *Ibid.*
13 *Ibid.*
14 *Ibid.*
15 *Ibid.*

Part II

On Witnessing

Sprich auch du,
sprich als letzter,
sag deinen Spruch.
Sprich—
Doch scheide das Nein nicht vom Ja.
Gib deinem Spruch auch den Sinn:
gib ihm den Schatten.
[...]
Blicke umber:
sieh, wie's lebendig wird rings—
Beim Tode! Lebendig!
Wahr spricht, wer Schatten spricht.

Speak, you too,
speak as the last one,
have your say.

Speak—
But do not separate the no from the yes.
Give your saying also meaning:
give it its shadow.
[...]
Look around:
see how alive it gets all around—
At death! Alive!
Speaks true, who speaks [of] shadows.

> Paul Celan, "Speak, you too", in *Memory Rose into Threshold Speech*,
> Joris, P. (Trans.), New York, Farrar, Straus and Giroux, 2020.

DOI: 10.4324/9781003435730-7

6

A Character, an Author, an Actor

A patient comes to see an analyst to find a remedy for his suffering. He speaks to the analyst. At first, things look like an exchange between two interlocutors, but soon the analyst notices that they are no longer alone. Other people have appeared in the office, which has turned into a theatre stage. These people demand that a play be written and directed. The analysis has started.

Pirandello's play *Six Characters in Search of an Author* can elucidate some of the basic elements of psychoanalytic psychotherapy. Six people enter a theatre and go up on the stage, where actors are rehearsing *The Rules of the Game*, another Pirandello play. These people demand that the Director write and stage their story, and he agrees. Taken aback but liberated and alive, the characters see their story being enacted by actors diverted from their initial roles.

This situation can serve to *represent* the practice of the analytic psychotherapist. "Doctor, is it serious?"

This question was an unexpected interruption of the flow in the tranquil narrative of a childhood memory that Christine was describing in a session. Until then, the therapist had been following comfortably the images of her early years as she unfolded them before him. But this question arose as suddenly as a storm in the mountains. The sky darkened in the blink of an eye. Suddenly dislodged from the position of a spectator where Christine had placed him, the analyst felt forced out of his orchestra seat, and invited to go up on stage, where a rehearsal was taking place. He was disconcerted.

Why was this question disturbing? After all, doesn't every patient have the right to ask his therapist this very question? Certainly, but the analyst had sensed that the question had not arisen naturally during the course of the patient's narrative. It had emerged inopportunely and had interrupted the flow of the session. In the guise of an innocent query, something new—or perhaps someone new—had appeared.

Taken aback, the therapist asked himself if this question required an answer. If he had answered that it was not serious, Christine would definitely not have believed him, and he pointed this out to her. Following Pirandello's example, he immediately asked all of Christine's relatives to make an appearance. He had known them a little ever since the first session when he had asked Christine to talk about her family—the living and the dead—but now he was inviting them to come on the

DOI: 10.4324/9781003435730-8

stage and make themselves comfortable. After contemplating them in silence for a time, he let the mother speak, lending her his voice:

—You look pale and tired, Christine. Please listen to me and have some rest... Go to bed, I'll prepare a hot water bottle.
—No, my mother didn't speak of hot water bottles, she offered to make me eggnog. Aside from that, it's exactly what she used to say. Often, when I was playing, my mother would come near me and look at me strangely, with a worried expression. And I would stop playing.

Clearly, the question that left the therapist speechless—"Is it serious?"—was the one her mother had implied just when Christine least expected it. The therapist, with Christine's help, was able to complete the question the mother did not know she was asking: "Do you have something serious? Could it be the serious kidney disease my brother had, which killed him when he was thirty and I was only twenty?"

Indeed, this question had never been formulated by Christine's mother. The nightmare of her brother's illness, which had marred her own childhood, had been banished from her consciousness. "He died and that was all". Determined to live "in reality", as she said, she had "turned the page". She asserted, in a peremptory tone, that she never thought about it, insisting loud and clear that "bygones are bygones". But those bygones were not gone and, unbeknownst to her, she had substituted her daughter for her brother. Christine was paying the price for the suffering her mother imagined she buried when her brother died.

By asking this question, Christine transmitted to the therapist what her body had recorded each time she was dislodged from her child's place, to be put in the place of an uncle who died too young, who was loved with a heart-wrenching love and secretly hated at the same time. Christine had made the analyst feel, and then translate, her displeasure when, at inopportune moments, her mother suggested that she needed rest, and even took her temperature and gave her some eggnog.

* * *

With Roberta, the analyst was faced with a situation in which his involvement was greater than in Christine's case. This time, he was going to reproduce, in a way, what had happened to Roberta. After he had unknowingly and unintentionally placed himself in the role of the patient's parents, he had to make an enormous psychic effort to regain his place as author–interpreter capable of helping her write the dramatic scenario of which she was the unsuspecting subject.

He had asked Robertaif they could set a different time for her session, but when she arrived at that time and rang the bell, he opened the door looking surprised and confused. Yes, it was the time set for her session, but he was with another patient. He was clearly distressed and he offered to set another time.

He had forgotten her—which was a serious error, he thought, especially in her case. He didn't know what would become of her psychoanalysis now. Would

Roberta put an end to an analysis conducted by such a forgetful therapist? To his great surprise, in the next session she found excuses for him and did not show any resentment. This attitude intrigued him. Roberta was making an effort to "understand" him, and minimised the effect this oversight had had on her. It was only when the analyst insisted that she admitted to herself what she had felt when she left his office: she felt obliterated. Her legs gave way and it took her time to be able to breathe again. When she got into her car, she knocked her face against the door and bruised herself.

For several days, the therapist felt only guilt when he thought of this incident, until he was able to picture it differently. Of course, he was the one who had forgotten, but didn't the patient play a part in this "oversight"? Had she not arranged things so that she would not be expected? Had something in her not insisted that she be forgotten again? Yes, that was it: she had succeeded in seducing her therapist, placing him on the stage of her childhood to play a character—the character representing the person who had not expected her. That was it, she had not been expected. And the words spoken in the next session: "You were not expected", brought to light a fact which had not been acknowledged until then. Both her parents had done everything possible to remain oblivious to the fact that they had not wanted their child, and worse, that they had not conceived it. And Roberta had helped them do this, she had contributed efficiently to this denial. The same inclination prompted her to find excuses for her therapist's slip, since she was used to understanding and excusing everything, pretending that "it never happened".

The analyst made it clear that he had been distressed, and admitted quickly that he had not forgotten the change in the hour set for the session. He also quickly admitted that it was his fault, that he was responsible for the mistake and that he had worried about the effects of this slip on his patient. In short, she had been on his mind, he was bearing her suffering.

As for her, she had also been able to do something she had never done in her childhood: belabour someone until something new emerged. "Belabour" suggests birth; indeed, this incident which might have seemed minor would take on the significance of a birth for Roberta.

For the analyst, the work consisted of coming down from the stage on which he let himself be summoned to mount. On that stage, he had told himself that he had forgotten her and felt guilty about it, but in fact he was playing the role of a "good enough parent". In a word, he was not embodying one of Roberta's murderous parents, but an adequate one. The productive reversal occurred when the analyst changed his subjective position and played once more the role of an author who could write Roberta's story: he offered her the chance of moving from the subjective position where she was the object of an "oversight" for which he took responsibility, to the subjective position of a child who was not expected. In this position, she was no longer only the object of denial, but was also the subject.

The fact that at the start the therapist felt guilty about the incident provided Roberta with an experience she never had in her childhood. Someone with whom she had a relationship had felt responsible for what happened, without blaming it on her from the start. In her family, everything was her fault, starting with the fact of being unloved, of being scorned and rejected. The process which revealed to her that she had always done her best to pretend, for her parent's sake, that she had been wanted by them, had allowed her to give a person responsible for her a feeling of remorse.

This experience shared with her analyst made it possible for Roberta to understand all the situations in her love life and social life when people had "forgotten" her. She was overlooked, disliked, considered a person without importance—all the symptoms afflicting her acquired meaning. Through her gestures, through her expressions, she was no doubt indicating a role to play—always the same role—to her partners. The therapist's real failing revealed the meaning of a childhood in which so many scenes signified the fact that she was unwanted. The experience shared with her therapist allowed her to glimpse the possibility that one day she would no longer have to play the role of an unwanted person. For the first time, someone had admitted that he had not expected her. In other words, he had accepted play a scene that had been recurring since time immemorial.

Little by little, changes took place in her life. She no longer felt obliged to keep alive her parents' illusion that they had wanted her, to assure them of the existence of a love they had never given her; she no longer felt she had to carry out the frightful task of proving to them that they loved her.

* * *

If the therapist had relied on his medical authority and told Christine that her anxieties were not serious, he would have indicated to her that he refused to consider her question relevant. Saying this would have meant that he decided to exclude this phrase from the patient's life narrative.

—Doctor, is it serious?
—How could it be? This can't be part of your story!

Such an answer would not only have excluded from the stage characters insearch of an author, but would also have indicated that there could no longer be a dramatic narration since at this very moment Christine was receiving attentive care from her therapist. Undoubtedly, the therapist had faith in the virtue of his strong suggestion and in his ability to put an end to that which had caused his patient's suffering. But beware: when he relies on this authority and erases the story of a character, he himself is unknowingly placed on the stage. Here, he would have taken up again the role of the mother who intended to erase the past. And the crisis would soon have flared up, in desperation as always, between the daughter and the therapist who thinks he is in his office in his street clothes, while the person she sees across her is her mother. In fact, it is when he most strongly holds on to his role as therapist that he is truly the mother, and then the *role* of the mother cannot be written or played. If he refuses to go on stage where the Daughter blindly beckons him, if he is determined to remain the protective therapist with the best intentions, he is not fulfilling his function as an author and director.

In Roberta's case, if the therapist would have apologised, he would have shown her that he made a mistake, that he admitted it, that he hoped Roberta would "understand" and that the therapy would continue as before. But at the same time, by presenting himself as a therapist who recognises his mistakes, he would have delivered Roberta into the hands of characters who refused to appear on the stage and who whispered her lines to her at the top of their voices from the wings. By inventing retort other than "I forgot about you", which his expression had immediately shown her, the analyst crossed over an obstacle for the second time, but in the opposite direction. The first time, as he could see now in hindsight, he found himself in the role of a well-meaning person who can admit his mistakes. The second time, the invention of a very different retort, "You were not expected", restored his function as an author. In the meantime, before returning to the function of author–interpreter, he had experienced, and endured, the situation of an uncaring character, despite himself. For a few days, he was in an uncomfortable position. Reversing it was difficult, because he had never imagined that he would one day find himself embodying such a hateful parent. When he crossed over the obstacle in the opposite direction, he gave life and consistency to all those who imputed to her a subjective position that they refused to recognise. Until then, she had been convinced that it was because she did not try hard enough that they did not love her. She was the one who felt guilty in their place. Now, the play that was being written gave back their roles to all the characters who had avoided them, with her complicity. Instead of the one-woman show she had painfully strived to perform until then, Roberta was now writing, session after session, with the help of the Director, a drama for several actors who had hitherto remained in the wings, with no story and no writing.

7

Near the Originary, Where
the Breath Fails

In this chapter I will elaborate on these strange occasions when, in my work as an analyst, I was knocked over and found myself unable to think and speechless, before finally—sometimes after a long time—being able to admit that I "repeated the crime", as Ferenczi put it.

To repeat the crime could have been, for example, not being there when the analysand was in a period of transition, when he was crossing over from a "before" to an "after", from a world which had been familiar to him to a world opening before him. Not having been there meant underestimating the risk for the subject at that moment in time, when he was ready to take the leap the analyst was encouraging him to take. By not being there at that moment, the analyst was stopping the momentum of the emerging subject, who had been supported until that time.

In these moments when the Real emerges—that which has no psychic inscription, has not found a place, and which Celan called the "intimate stranger"—when it emerges unexpectedly—and it never emerges otherwise—the analyst that I am always found himself at a loss. So that later, when I had eliminated the figure of an inverted transference, that is, in a scene where I was relegated to the place of the *infans* mistreated by the analysand in the role of a parent, I had to face the fact that I had once again been swept off the stage and into a black hole, speechless.

Henri Maldiney's work is of help in my reflections on these transferential events which carry me off to this no-place without inscription where I betray the analysand and seem to be betrayed myself, since I feel painfully surprised by my own failing. On these shores, the poets are our teachers, and as far as "one's own" is concerned, Hölderlin reminds us that one's "ownmost" is the most foreign:

> To be able to make free use of one's "ownmost", [...] admittedly requires a confrontation with the foreign. Spirit must therefore venture into the foreign, [...] to make itself ready [...] for what is its own. [...] One's own is what is most difficult to find.[1]

Indeed, nothing is as close to us *and* nothing is our ownmost as much as this unexpected thing at the core of our being, the unconscious. I am not speaking here of the unconscious as a reservoir of repressed representations, but rather of the

DOI: 10.4324/9781003435730-9

unknowable core, the hiatus between the Id and the Ego, which eludes thematisa-
tion and is, at the same time, the necessary condition of reflexivity, as Nicolas
Abraham[2] points out.

But what exactly is the nature of this learning "difficult to find" when there can
be no objective knowledge of what is at stake. The object we speak of *does not*
actually exist, it *is* not. Knowledge acquired through experience, so highly praised
by Aeschylus in *Agamemnon*, has to be put in perspective. This kind of learning is
not complete. At best, it can serve to re-cognise the premonitory phase or the aura
of the object. Here, learning means acquiring the ability to be alerted by the signs—
anguish first and foremost—announcing the absence of signs; imminent defeat.

> Every whole appears in a living point of view and all that exists is internally
> divided. Nature cannot appear in its original strength but needs art as something
> weaker than itself in order to appear. But in art, nature does not appear originally
> but through the mediation of a sign, i.e. the hero. As such a sign, [...] insig-
> nificant and without effect. [...] But when [...] the sign is equal to zero (total
> collapse), [...] the hidden foundation of any nature, can also present itself [...]
> in its most powerful gift.[3]

To tell the truth, my ability to consent to the shock of this unforeseen/unpre-
cedented thing which sometimes repeats itself and grabs hold of me by surprise—
this willingness is what makes me an analyst with certain patients. This is what Bion
means when he speaks of the analyst's capacity for breakdown. I understand this capacity to be the willingness of the analyst to let himself be taken back to the brink of
breakdown, where one gasps for breath, at the edge of the bottomless depth on which
he undertakes to build. To paraphrase Paul Celan in *The Meridian* (Breathturn):

> Only when with your most own pain [...] And then you stand with your falling
> silent thinking in the pause which reminds you of your heart, and don't speak of
> it. And speak later of yourself.[4]

And it is only later that you "speak in matters concerning you". Much later, after
the inscription of a word perhaps, "ventured in self-forgetfulness", which provides
the thing with its negative aspect and gives it its shadow. Yes, it can be a word,
but the inscription can also be that of a silence.

> ... most painfully mindful of all the experiences and shocks [*Erschütterun-
> gen*] we write ourselves toward a necessary, inalienable [*unabdingbar*] reality
> [*Wirklichen*] —: in word-shape — what else could it be?—, open on all sides,
> we venture, and that is at times unpleasant, into the word — and answerless".[5]

In this fragment taken from Celan's Drafts for his Buchner Prize acceptance speech,
he says: "We write ourselves...". This "ourselves" designates an "I" and a "me".
I write myself, I write from my openness to this *Wirklichkeit*, this efficient reality,

this real which is my foundation, which keeps escaping me and sometimes betrays me. It is when I can breathe again, after being subjected to the assault of the real once again, that I come back to myself—an event equivalent to an advent. Henri Maldiney defined an event–advent in these terms: "The event is what grabs me by surprise", scrambles all the signs and "opens the world". This event is "transformative and [is only received] to transform us".[6] Maldiney assigns the word "reality" to this lightning flash occurring in the being, this event–advent. Like a rebirth, something new emerges, provided I acquiesce to the event to which the analysand invites me, an advent to which I did not know I was summoned. For his part, at the time of this advent the analysand is no longer the monster he thought he was. Maldiney reminds us that "monster" comes from *monere*, to warn. The analysand, who in his childhood was constantly warning his parent about the dissonant character of one attitude or another, only to have his warnings systematically brushed aside, sees a curtain finally lifting. And the monster he was melts away.

In this zone of transitional phenomena, which Maldiney and Jean Oury, following in the footsteps of Francis Ponge, called a "pre" zone—prior to and outside of any representation, prior to and outside of any perception, any distinction between inside and outside—in this zone of the pathic, before the *logos*, the first meaningful sense of the word "reality" is "unsignifiable meaning", which presents itself as a "desire to say" with which the *infans* comes to knock at the door of the world when a rhythm compatible with life has carried him until then.

> There is a universal meaning for which we thirst. [...] Poetry is a constant renewal of language. It keeps alive in language a thirst for what is native. What distinguishes the poet is a thirst for coming-to-life together, the thirst for a word born with the world.[7]

This thirst for meaning, this dynamic set in place by this impulse to participate, as Erwin Straus called it—this thirst which precedes the appetite for wanting to say, to put into words—enables me to embody the notion of psychic matrix I proposed some years ago. By transitional psychic matrix, I mean the semiotic envelope created when the parent "dreams" the child she expects. This envelope is woven virtually from all word–thing dualities. It makes place for nothingness, for the unexpected, but at times it presents a gap in which the thing is missing its consort, the word. At such times the *infans* unfailingly directs himself towards this gap, this blind and deaf spot in the envelope where inscription is lacking. The thing is missing its negative aspect and consequently has no existence. The child, seduced by this void like a moth by a light bulb, draws his parent's attention by exhibiting a symptom in the blind hope of seeing "the thing" come into existence, in order to be freed from this place to which he is unknowingly assigned. He does not know that he is waiting for his parent to free him, to make the thing exist by recognising it—not so much because naming it would give it its negativity and would make it something shared with the parent, with which the child could play—but above all because this recognition would appease the conflict in which the parent engages with himself. This appeasement would put an end to the rhythmic dissonance between the languages the parent speaks to the child. The same is true for the analysand, who could find himself suddenly taken back to the black sun of this blind and deaf strip of the past, if I hesitate to recognise—once again—"earth's horror that entraps his feathers".

His neck will shake off this whitest agony
Space inflicts on a bird that denies it wholly,
But not earth's horror that entraps his feathers.
Phantom assigned to this place by his brilliance
[…].[8]

Indeed, the analysis of a patient who had been seduced by a blind and deaf space, without writing and deprived of the psychic matrix in which the parent envelops the baby—with no objection or compensatory act from the other parent—such an analysis will find its place in this zone of the originary, in the zone of the analyst's groundlessness. This space left blank by something censored, by a crime, a hidden catastrophe, scandalous and shameful, a thing that doesn't exist but insists, this space hides, obliterates the unthinkable associated with finitude which, for its part, is celebrated in rituals and is shared by all human beings.

When the child was assigned to the place outside the door of a room not figuring on the plans of his house, the analysis takes place outside the closed-off room in the analyst's house, in the virtual space formed between his Id and his Ego, and the outcome depends on the analyst's analysis, not on his capacity for breakdown, as Bion says, [9] but on his ability to ground himself, without collapsing, on his own bottomless depth, sometimes after having "repeated the crime" and admitted it. The subject in the analyst becomes himself, just as the subject in the analysand does. Here, speaking of the subject means speaking of the core of the being, between Id and Ego, disposed, or not, to let itself catch another glimpse of the catastrophe on which it is grounded.

The word "reality" itself is asleep. It is rendered ordinary by language, worn down by the abuses of language, the worst of which is the most common. […] Reality is an unsignifying significance. We only experience it when we are struck dumb. […] It appears suddenly in an event that scrambles all the signs. An event-advent does not take place in the world. All the systems in operation until then collapse. The event is transformative and we can only take it in if we are transformed ourselves. […] When the lightning flash of an event tears the fabric of my world.[10]

The same is true of analysis.

In its auto-sublation it sees its—perhaps only—chance […] In this in-between, the space of its becoming free, its being set free and floating free, *in statu nascendi* thus, and simultaneously also *in statu moriendi*, lies the ground of the poem. This groundlessness the poem takes as its ground (set as its ground).[11]

"And only later [you] speak of yourself". Later, after an inscription, or even without a word ventured. To return to Celan's "we write ourselves", I shall go back to *A Project for a Scientific Psychology*, where Freud has a brilliant perception of dual unity when he describes the phenomenology of the originary, the coming into being which involves the *infans* and his fellow-creature, the *Nebenmensch*. In a passage about judging, [12] Freud speaks of the human being (the *infans*) who recognises his own hands, his own screams, by *perceiving* the hands, the scream, of the human being next to him.

Henri Maldiney focuses on a level before perception, in the zone of the pathic, where sensation combines with movement, *aesthesis* with *kinaesthesis*, apart from perception. In one of his essays, Jérôme de Gramont observed that Maldiney's phenomenology originates in sensation, while Merleau-Ponty's, and Freud's before him, originated in perception, in the zone of the *percipiens*, what is felt. This perception presupposes the existence of space and time, a distinction between inside and outside, between subject and object. Maldiney's reasoning is grounded on rhythm, when he speaks of the originary. This is, in part, what explains my affinity with Maldiney's writing.

> A rhythm […] is grounded on sensation, which grounds it by giving it shape. This shape only exists as a becoming. Its rhythmic self-generation creates space and time.[13]

In Maldiney's writing, form and rhythm are associated in the work of conceiving the subject, a form in constant formation.

> [Rhythm] creates the place where opposites communicate. […] [In rhythm] the conflict between closed and open, as well as its resolution, does not occur at a specific point in the shaping, but at each point of its self-generation.[14]

Writing about Maldiney, Jean-Marc Ghitti adds:

> ... rhythm is the staging of movement. It connects chaos and space dialectically. Rhythm's own time is a succession of responses through which it lifts itself out of natural repetitivity and saves itself from collapsing into chaos.[15]

I am convinced that the condition necessary for the *infans* to recognise his scream, his pain, his hand, so that the scream, the hands, all the parts of his body and all his functions, all affects can be inscribed in him—this condition is that the *Nebenmensch* remain in rhythmic concertation with him. I see this concertation as being the basis of what Maldiney calls transpassibility. Rhythm is the way in which the one "next to" the child shows that he is there and that he can be there again, or be there no matter what, even when what happens is unforeseeable and unprecedented. The *Nebenmensch* is open to any possibility, he is grounded on Nothingness. His lightness comes from his knowledge and his tolerance of the groundlessness on which he is grounded, with which he made a pact. He is used to being summoned by the *infans*, who shows him what path to avoid, what direction not to take, like Balaam's donkey did, even when he whipped her when she refused to continue in the wrong direction.[16]

Freud must be given credit for having had the intuition, at the end of his life, when his theoretical edifice had been built, that rhythm is the *primum movens* in the formation of the subject. In 1924, in his article "The Economic Problem of Masochism", he wrote:

> It appears that [pleasure and unpleasure] depend, not on this quantitative factor, but on some characteristic of it which we can only describe as a qualitative one. If we were able to say what this qualitative characteristic is, we should be much further advanced in psychology. Perhaps it is the rhythm, the temporal sequence of changes, rises and falls in the quantity of stimulus. We do not know.[17]

The one who answers for the infans, on the brink of collapse where he stands on groundlessness, capable of incapacity, capable of existing in unknowing, gives the gift of closure, and donates what Freud called primal repression. The *chora*, the *makom*, Lacan's split subject, the virtual bridge between the Id and the Ego, is created by the attention paid by the *Nebenmensch* and by the rhythmic response it restores after a discontinuity. This bridge spans the space between the edges of the gap that opens, at the same time, between the Id and the Ego. The bridge is part of the subject's nature; they are born at the same time. The bridge is the representation of the assurance given to the Id that it will find its Ego on the other side of a gap that he ventures to leap over. "The only remedy for dizziness is rhythm".[18]

The interaction between the *Nebenmensch* and the *infans* is the psycho-corporal process that creates the *chora*, the virtual place imagined by Plato where opposites can exist together; the *Makom*, one of the names of God in the Jewish tradition; Winnicott's "self"; Lacan's metaphor of the split subject; Maldiney's closed and open space of the subject characterised by transpassibility. Such a place is the form called forth by the field of tension of a rhythm in which closed and open alternate, a discontinuous rhythm "whose flow is never flawless", [19] but is adopted by the infant, so that "the human being beside him" takes it up in an "expected–unexpected" echo. In my view, this expected–unexpected response is the paradigm of the pleasure the child takes in continuing to explore the world. Creativity finds nourishment and renewed vitality in this pleasure to respond, in the restored rhythm of the breath after an interruption.

When the "human being next to him" does not take up the rhythm set by the infant's chorus, when he doesn't find the rhythm after a rhythmic discontinuity he does not notice, or ignores, or actively denies, primal repression is damaged, altered, gaping. This gap is antithetical to "the Open" Maldiney references.[20] Thus, when the break in the rhythm is not repaired, the parent's deficiency, or the defence he builds against it, is "sucked in" as a makeshift filler to plug the gap that has been created. This is how unknown ghosts and pains survive in the infant, unavoidable consequences of the dual unit, illustrated by Kafka's short story "The Vulture", which I read as a parable of incorporation.

I consider this a seminal text not only because it offers a poetic description of an aggressor, but also because it portrays orgastic scansion. Kafka points out the orgastic nature of the moment when the subject swallows the one who torments him. He does this to survive. This point is crucial because it reveals the nonspecific character of the sexual, given that orgastic pleasure is the mark of both introjection and incorporation. Not taking into account that the sexual is the factotum of organo-psychic life explains the failure of analysis in many cases.

The *infans* who swallows his tormentor has to propel himself headlong onto the other side of the gap, has to become a bridge himself to connect the two edges of the gap, in order to avoid sinking into the bottomless depth, to avoid collapsing.

"I was stiff and cold, I was a bridge, I lay over a ravine. [...] So I lay and waited; I could only wait. Without falling, no bridge, once spanned, can cease to be a bridge." One day, the bridge heard a man coming and prepared itself to support him and enable him to get to the other side. But when the passenger arrived, first he plunged the point of his stick into the bridge's bushy hair, and then he jumped with both feet on the middle of his body, causing him atrocious pain. Who was it?, the bridge asked himself. "A child? A dream? A wayfarer? A suicide? A tempter? A destroyer?" He turned around to see him. But a bridge to turn around! He had not quite finished turning when he began to fall, and in a moment he was "torn and transpierced by the sharp rocks which had always gazed up at me so peacefully from the rushing water".[21]

My refusal to be there at times, the withdrawal of the "human being nearby" whom I had been until then, the time it takes me to recognise this withdrawal—all cause the analysand to gasp for breath. The shortness of breath caused by the effects of my blind spot—Michael Balint spoke of "basic fault"[22]—produces rhythmic dissonance. When I don't take up the rhythm again, when I refuse to recognise the absurdity of my attitude towards the patient, he can react either by ending the analysis or by incorporating my failing.

For the infant, and for the infant in the analysand, it is a miracle to see someone testify to the relevance of the demand he addressed to me, and to have his impression that there is a forbidden place in the analyst confirmed. It is miraculous to feel that one's parent or analyst lives with a deaf zone, a gap. The miracle is to take part in the creation of the world, to see the tearing of a veil which brings into existence something that life was missing until then, extracts it from the void where it was waiting for its chance to exist. "Artistic creation is also a miracle of sorts".[23] It is a miracle to be the inventor of a blind and deaf zone in the one who acts as a parent—the analyst. It is a miracle for the analysand to see his discovery confirmed and validated. Du Bouchet says that you only enter the world if you disappeared.

Disappeared? Who disappeared in this process? No one, except the image of the practitioner in me who thought he was the ideal analyst, flawless, blameless, who never lacked attention and never sought vengeance when he was contradicted, mistreated, or attacked. After all, I had not set out on this path, that of analysis, without the secret wish to see this thing, this unexpected/unprecedented thing, forgotten once and for all, without wishing secretly never to face it again. But the fact is that in one analysis or another I risk having brought to light the dark matter, the blind spot of my being, the place where I am voiceless. Once again I have to admit that I have fallen into the trap set by the analysand and the characters in search of an author who, on my side and his, emerge to tell their story. I have wounded the analysand and I admitted it. The miracle is that thanks to this admission, "the enormity of the emergence rips the world apart".[24] A veil is torn, another world appears.

Notes

1 Hölderlin, F., "Letter to Böhlendorf", in Benjamin, W., *Selected Writings, Vol. 3, 1935–1938*, Cambridge, MA, Harvard University Press, 2002.
2 Abraham, N. and Torok, M., *The Shell and the Kernel*, Chicago, IL, University of Chicago Press, 1994.
3 Hölderlin, F., *Selected Writings, Vol. 3, 1935–1938*, op. cit.
4 Celan, P., *The Meridian, Final Version—Drafts—Materials*, Stanford, CA, Stanford University Press, 2011, p. 127.
5 *Ibid.*, p. 66.
6 Maldiney, H., *L'Art, l'éclair de l'être* [Art, the Lightning of Being], Seyssel, *Éditions Comp'Act, 2003.*
7 *Ibid.*
8 Mallarmé, S., "The Virginal, Vibrant, and Beautiful Dawn", in *Collected Poems*, Weinfield, H. (Trans.), Berkeley, CA, University of California Press, 2011, p. 67.
9 Bion, W., *Elements of Psychoanalysis*, Oxford, Routledge, 1984.
10 Maldiney, H., *L'Art, l'éclair de l'être*, op. cit.
11 Celan, P., *The Méridian: Final Version—Drafts—Materials*, op. cit. p.60.
12 Freud, S., *A Project for a Scientific Psychology*, S.E. 1, London: Hogarth.
13 Maldiney, H., *Penser l'homme et la folie*, Grenoble, Éditions Jérôme Millon, 1997.
14 See, *acontrario*, the rhythm without resolution of Schreber's "talking birds". Maldiney, H., *Regard, parole, espace*, Lausanne, Âge d'homme, 1994.
15 Ghitti, J.-M., "Maldiney, du chaos à l'espace'", in Younès, C. and Frérot, O. (Eds.), *À l'épreuve d'exister avec Henri Maldiney*, Paris, Hermann, 2016.
16 Numbers, 22.
17 Freud, S., *The Economic Problem of Masochism*, S.E. 19, London: Hogarth.
18 Maldiney, H., *Existence, crise et création*, Versanne, Encre Marine, 2001.
19 Maldiney, H., *Penser l'homme et la folie*, op. cit.
20 Maldiney, H., *L'Art, l'éclair de l'être*, op. cit.
21 Kafka, F., "The Bridge", in *Collected Stories*, Muir, W. and Muir, E. (Trans.), New York, Alfred A. Knopf, 1993.
22 Balint, M., *The Basic Fault*, Evanston, IL, Northwestern University Press, 1992.
23 Malevitch, K., quoted by Henri Maldiney in *Art et existence*, op. cit.
24 Ghitti, J.-M., "Maldiney, du chaos à l'espace'", op. cit.

8

The Theory of Hysteria Hindered by the Absence of a Witness

[In] a Hungarian village [...] the blacksmith had been guilty of a capital offence. The burgomaster, however, decided that as a penalty, a tailor should be hanged and not the blacksmith, because there were two tailors in the village but no second blacksmith, and the crime must be expiated.

Sigmund Freud, *Jokes and Their Relation to the Unconscious*

During a session that was crucial for a particular analysand, the analyst became absent when he nodded off briefly. This would not have been especially noteworthy had he not felt intense guilt for having fallen asleep just when the patient was recounting an episode of her psychic life that had been an important turning point for her. When he awakened, he had felt grabbed by the throat, petrified, neutralised. He was speechless. Intent on his silent effort to save face, he pretended that nothing happened. And this "as if it never happened" transformed him, for a long time, into an impassive individual of the species *homo psychanalyticus*.

Instead of saying to himself, as he was used to doing, that in the scene which had unfolded "someone" had failed to pay attention, he took responsibility for it, making it his "fault". Instead of thinking that the fact that he nodded off just then indicated that this absence was—not only, but also—the repetition of an absence experienced by the patient as a child, which she had since carried within her, the analyst had gone up on the stage where his analysand summoned him. He had answered the call of the siren. To use Pirandello's metaphor about "characters in search of an author", instead of writing the scene, the analyst became one of the characters of the play. He had moved to another place and had used his lapse to illustrate his feeling of guilt, which was always ready to emerge.

Then, one day, the analyst was ready to consider that, despite himself, he had set in place the conditions for mutual analysis. In the course of this analysis, he was obliged to recognise—at length and despite great reluctance—all the elements of a tragic event that marked the start of his practice, which was only known to a few people close to him, and which he had buried under a cement slab, as is done with a nuclear reactor out of control. His dreams described in detail the circumstances of this tragedy, where 35 years ago, in the middle of a session, a patient attempted suicide and only survived thanks to a miracle.

DOI: 10.4324/9781003435730-10

The figure of the witness is among those essential to the parental function. In the economy of sensations, the parent is required to stand witness on several levels. First, he creates the sensation: by interpreting a scream, crying, certain movements, he introduces the child to the universe of signs, he establishes his sensation, attests to it. He then acts as a witness by connecting the child's sensation to a specific event, and finally by helping to inscribe the event into a sequence that links past, present and future. At each of these stages a failing can occur; the younger the child concerned, the greater its consequences will be.

A sensation comes into being provided the child finds next to him a witness who becomes the messenger between his body and his psyche. In the absence of such a witness, only the body keeps a record of the blocked out event. A certain analysand is not aware that he is cold, another doesn't perceive pain. An analysand who never knew when she was hungry led me to understand that her obesity was related to the fact that she doesn't experience hunger. Her mother only fed her to reduce her own anxiety, she did not wait for a sign from the baby, a sign for her to interpret, that she could have understood as the baby's hunger. This mother's anxiety inhibited the sensation that otherwise the psychic matrix in which she carried her child would have allowed her to call "hunger".

A parent who has experienced a feeling—pain or shame for example—but who refuses to put it into words, produces what we can call hysterical suffering in the child. I think it appropriate to speak in these terms because in a letter to Wilhelm Fliess dated December 6, 1896, Freud speaks of repression as the effect of a "refusal to retranscribe" (*Versagung der Übersetzung*).[1] Freud considers this repression the effect of censoring the subject, but I am convinced that the child perceives the parent's refusal to acknowledge one of his own sensations, and he adjusts to this refusal. This perspective agrees with the understanding of the early Freud—the one who elaborated trauma theory—concerning the economy of unavowed suffering between parent and child. But the failing of the witness can sometimes be of a different nature. I am speaking of instances when this failing leads to soul murder. In the example of the little boy rescued by his parents from the psychic agony into which they propelled him—they had unexpectedly improvised a hide-and-seek game to enjoy seeing his terror—these parents committed soul murder. They deprived the child of a foundational event, since after the erasure of consciousness inflicted on him, he invents himself as a new subject with a new origin. The event remains unwitnessed since the child was lifeless when the blow struck him, and since the parents do not know they committed this crime. As a result, the child will remain a stranger to himself because his place of origin has shifted. As for the parents, they will no longer recognise their child, whose behaviour seems strange to them. Banished from his own unique origin, this child cannot turn back on himself, any more than he can turn to look at his parents, whom he saw as his saviourswhen he came out of the psychic agony they inflicted on him. This scene, paradigmatic of soul murder, can occur much earlier in a child's life, when he is in the position of "unconditional hostage", the very apt term invented by Emmanuel Levinas to refer to the radical passivity of human beings at the start of their lives. When the witness in the child has been mistreated in this manner, the new subject who emerges often displays borderline characteristics.

Don Juan is the paradigm of these beings who were subjected to soul murder and who ceaselessly repeat the movement driving them towards a mirror, but only so that they can break it as soon as they find it. They run away as soon as someone is in a position to discover that their image is that of a child left for dead. Don Juan flees when a woman is about to discover that he cannot see himself, or, to use a literary metaphor, that he has no shadow. Don Juan cannot see himself because his strange origin is unknown to him, because the soul murder he suffered has erased the trace of death with which his parents had endowed him at birth.

The trace of death, a founding element in constituting a human being, consists of the objection to death which the parents made for the child at his birth, and which they renew for him in many different ways. This objection is evident first in the clear caesura which punctuate the sensorial solicitations the mother addresses to the child. This aporetic sequence of incitation and withholding is the condition necessary to give the subject a shadow, so that he can see his image in the mirror provided by someone else. The quality of this sequence will determine the quality of the relations the subject establishes with other people.

Don Juan, on the other hand, enters into a make-believe relation with another, some sort of relation, but he is unable to establish a reciprocal relation in which two equal individuals facing each other, adversaries—*ad versum*—decide to undertake a shared experience. Instead, he pretends he has a shadow and becomes the awakener, the protector or the tyrant of the one he meets. In contrast to Don Juan, another person who suffered the same fate could be servile and completely exploitable—but it comes to the same thing.

The question of witnessing does not apply in the same way to Don Juan as it does to Ferline or Masetto. They do not adopt the same perspective. When confronted with an event, Don Juan does not refuse to testify because, from his standpoint, nothing happened. He is sincere when he lies, and in good faith when he refuses to take responsibility. No fact that contradicts the luminous being he is, no event that contradicts his view of the world, which in his opinion is only Light, can exist. "No fuss" is the motto of this wounded man who declares that there is nothing to look for behind words or in dreams.[2]

The theory of hysteria, the corpus of Freud's oeuvre, starts with the encounter between a "child with all his impulses"[3] and a child in whom the witness has been destroyed. The theory of hysteria originates in the seductive effect that a Don Juan of the world of science exerted over Freud. In this foundational scene, a genius whose curiosity was insatiable was seduced by a man without a shadow, a wounded man filled with an irrepressible impatience to explain everything.

Between 1893 and 1899, in the period when Fliess was his only important interlocutor, Freud entered a feverish state of unbelievable creativity in which his ideas extended to new fields, elucidated from novel perspectives. In that period, he opened four new paths, in addition to that of dreams, which he would explore for 15 years without exhausting their possibilities. Within a few months, *Sexuality in the Aetiology of the Neuroses, The Psychopathology of Everyday Life, Jokes* and *Metapsychology* opened new directions for exploration. But during the same period there was a reversal in Freud's conception of hysteria. It was nothing spectacular, but the focus shifted to the hysteric's perspective: the position from which he sees and hears himself. This perspective, instead of being internal–external to the subject, became exclusively internal. My hypothesis is that this shift was related to the catastrophic ending of Freud's friendship with Fliess.[4]

In my view, what seduced Freud about Fliess between 1893 and 1895 was the impression of total security emanating from a person who feels infallible and who succeeds at whatever he undertakes. Fliess's daring theoretical and clinical feats are renowned. In Germany, *mil e tre* patients run to see him to be treated for gynecological annoyances by having their nostrils cauterised with trichloracetic acid or with vinegar. His theoretical research is promising; he has developed a new theory based on biological principles applicable to all living species—just as all celestial bodies obey Kepler's laws. Fliess offers Freud the confidence of a man free of the smallest doubt, afraid of nothing and, with this confidence, ready to obey the laws of the world—in this case, the laws governing a scientific project worthy of the name. Fliess advises Freud, treats him, cures him of his headaches and his precordial pain, and of the *taedium vitae* that plagues him. Above all, Fliess holds Freud in his power by keeping alive his friend's belief that he, Fliess, can predict the dates when Sigmund could die.

Fliess has all the characteristics of those who were subjected to murder of the soul in their childhood, and became either tyrants or slaves. Fliess embodies the figure of the tyrant who has found, through the exercise of a practice resembling magic, a way of wielding power. He treats words as if they were things[5] and hides the despair which, unbeknownst to him, drives his frantic quest for a grandiose "scientific" discovery, for the sake of which the end justifies the means. This magician has found in Freud a researcher initiating a revolution whose outcome he feels is very uncertain. Like all wounded individuals who become deniers of the crime to which they were subjected, Fliess found in Freud an entirely living person who is affected—even deeply moved—by the praise or the threats proffered by the magician. The unfeeling Fliess has found in Freud someone he can "possess", as a shell finds a hermit crab, or a cage finds its bird.[6]

Every clinician is familiar with the figure of a parent who has a child as a way to survive, even though he has given up what is essential, and despite the fact that the ethical spring of his existence is broken. A living-dead parent has a child in order to take refuge in him. With Freud, Fliess acts like the parent who, in order to survive his psychic death, holds onto the child, turning him into his possession. Freud is a prolific thinker, and his ideas are addressed to Fliess. It is to him that sublime letters are sent, as well as an ambitious proposal for a scientific psychology still consulted by researchers today. Fliess kept them faithfully.[7] He gave himself life through Freud by making himself his irreplaceable protector. He arranged for Freud to be unable to do without him, and kept him in his power by protecting him from a death that his calculations predicted.

The catastrophic ending of this friendship and of the professional collaboration on which it was founded occurred in three stages, which led to the emergence of the new theory of hysteria. The first stage took place in 1895, when Fliess refused to admit making a professional error. The second stage took place in 1898, when Freud and his friend refused to acknowledge that Fliess's research was rejected by the scientific community. The third stage consisted of censuring Freud's specimen dream. At each stage, Freud acted *as if nothing happened*, as if these events were not serious. At the last stage—the last act of the play—he writes *The Interpretation of Dreams*, in which he sacrifices trauma theory, covering up the lack of a witness who refuses to recognise specific events.

The first act is where Emma Eckstein appears between Freud and Fliess. Breuer recommended this patient to Freud, who entrusted her to Fliess to relieve her of stomach pains which Fliess claimed to cure by removing a portion of the nasal turbinet. Fliess operated on Emma in February 1895, and left a length of gauze in her nasal cavity. Performing a second operation became urgent in March, since Emma's general state of health had worsened and a putrid odour was emanating from the wound. The surgery caused severe hemorrhage and vascular collapse, treated just in time. Fliess insisted that he bore no responsibility and maintained this position in the months and years that followed. He never admitted that negligence, at the very least, could be attributed to him in these tragic events. His excuses were ludicrous: the gauze was of poor quality and the ORL specialist called urgently should not have operated in Emma's home. Fliess went as far as demanding that Freud obtain a certificate freeing him of blame, from the holder of the Chair of ORL in Vienna. He also expected Freud to provide him with the dates of Emma's menstrual cycle, as well as her history as it emerged in her analysis, in order to put together proof of haemophilia or hysteria.

Freud accepts his friend's demands and interprets Emma's dreams, fantasies and memories in the light requested by Fliess. This submission blinds him to what Emma's dreams and fantasies, and his own, reveal. As for Emma, her dreams are clearly a search for witnesses who can testify to what she has undergone. She dreams that the Devil sticks pins in her fingers and then places a candy on each drop of blood. In his letter to Fliess dated January 17, 1897, Freud takes advantage of this image to make a comment which reads like a recognition of the link between Emma's fantasy and Fliess's error, and at the same time like the covering up of this error: "As far as the blood is concerned, you are completely without blame!" The letter also speaks of a "foreign body", and asserts that "once more the Inquisitors prick with needles, to discover the Devil's stigmata".[8]

When Freud does not recognise the "foreign body" as the gauze which almost cost Emma her life and might have also cost him a good part of his reputation in Vienna, when he does not recogniseFliess and himself in the "Inquisitors", and he does not see his patient's fantasy as a representation of the harassment he is inflicting on her in order to exonerate at all costs his scalpel and bone clamp-wielding friend, he allies himself with a "bungler of souls".[9] This resonance remains present in the first chapter of his masterpiece—a clinical chapter—since he chooses as his specimen dream "Irma's injection", a faithful dream representation of this drama. But Freud doesn't comment on the appeals Emma launches in his own dream; he declares that after having explored some of the significant options open to him, he prefers not to explore others, and finally he asks the reader to agree that it is impossible to say everything when analysing one's own dreams. He concludes the chapter by telling the story of the man who borrows a kettle and refutes his neighbour's accusation that he gave it back with a hole in it. The man argues in his own defence that he gave back the kettle undamaged, that the kettle already had a hole when he borrowed it, and in the end, devil take it all, he never borrowed the kettle. By telling this story, Freud launches an appeal. He calls for witnesses in order to make possible the reopening of an investigation after he unconsciously made evidence related to it disappear.

But Freud had already abandoned trauma theory, also called seduction theory, in favour of a theory of "seduction fantasies". In this new theory of hysteria, an endogenous seducer—the libido—replaced an external seducer. The new theory reads like the defence Fliess could have presented in court if the Eckstein family had brought charges against him. "Emma's bleeding is caused by *Sehnsucht*, longing; the causes of her illness are internal, they are related to her libidinal economy", maintains the man who refuses to admit his surgical error.

The birth certificate of this theory is signed by three protagonists: Freud, Emma Eckstein and Fliess, all of whom introduce—each for their own unconscious reason—a flawed witness into the foundations of psychoanalysis. This flawed witness buried under the bearing wall of the new edifice would become an invisible seducer and was going to conduct the analyses of Dora and the Wolf Man, model patients who underwent what many more patients would experience in those years and in the future.[10]

To please the host of a dead witness whose motto is: "No need to make a fuss, nothing happened", Freud created a system that subsumed the pathological within the normal, the traumatic within the universal and the fragmented within the continuous. To confer coherence to this operation which erases an event just as a star is sucked into a black hole, Freud invites two prestigious figures to place a gift in the cradle of psychoanalysis. Jocasta, a false witness *par excellence*, places her famous authoritative *proton pseudos* in the cradle: "What man, in his dreams, has not shared his mother's bed?" The second figure, Auguste Comte, offers up Broussais's principle, developed a few decades earlier, which had become the central concept of the positivism adopted by men of science in the late 19th century. This principle: "The differences between the normal and the pathological are only a matter of degree", is the bridgehead that made possible the passage of Fliess's ideas into Freud's system of thinking. Jocasta and Auguste Comte are the two proponents of an endogenous sexual phenomenon, traumatic *in principio*.

This submersion of the traumatic under the deluge of the normal was related to Freud's need to deal with the man who denied all responsibility of the harm done to Emma. To protect his magician healer and avoid acknowledging his own complicity in the assault suffered by Emma Eckstein, Freud was sacrificing the theory which allowed him to read her fantasies and his own dreams. In this situation, Freud acted like all those who cannot confront a parent, a friend or even a psychoanalyst when this person is responsible for an error, a blunder, a fault.

Forced silence about a refusal to recognise a part of reality, a refusal of translation, was turning Freud away from the paths that would have allowed him to understand the meaning of his dream and of Emma's unconscious productions. Like all hysterics, Emma only had her fantasies—that is, coded messages like those Freud had learned to decode like a true Champollion—to signal an ethical failing to her therapist. Given that they are "unconditional hostages", the *infans* and later the *infans* in the analysand only have their unconscious productions, fantasies, dreams and their bodies to signify such a failing. They can only confront the parent or the analyst if they are given tacit permission to do so. If a child encounters very early his parents' refusal to see or hear, he is left to deal with the lack of witnessing alone. The way he deals with it always consists of "understanding". He tries to understand his parent and he succeeds. In analysis, the same thing will happen; it will always be through unconscious productions that the analysand will point out to the analyst the mistake or blunder he committed. Emma's fantasies, as Freud describes them in his letter dated January 17, 1897, are a good example of this.[11]

The second stage of the foundation of the new theory of hysteria occurs when the consequences of a catastrophe unfold—a catastrophe involving both Freud and Fliess, although the latter is more directly concerned. In April 1898, a newspaper critic wrote a scathing review of Fliess's book *The Relations between the Nose and the Female Sexual Organs*. Ry, the critic, asserted that none of the results of Fliess's nasal experiments were validated in Viennese clinics and hospitals where studies were conducted, and that, moreover, it was "useless to submit his theories on masculine and feminine series to serious refutation since, like the practical applications of nasal and periodic theories, they are nothing but disgusting drivel". The article concludes: "It is a wonder that after a few pages the reader doesn't get the feeling that the author is making a mockery of him".[12] Seeing this massacre, Freud expressed his shock to his friend, stopped his subscription to the newspaper, but did not want to incite controversy and defend Fliess's ideas and therapeutic practices. He continued his collaboration with Fliess and acted *as if nothing happened*, as if the scientific community had not refused to recognise the value of Fliess's work.

The third stage of the foundation was enacted one month after the publication of this disastrous article. In May 1898, Freud sent Fliess his *grosseTraum* (Big Dream), which he considered the paradigm of all his dreams, saying he "analysed it meticulously and completely". Why does Fliess forbid him to publish it? Freud asks him whether the topic to which he objected was "my anxiety, or Martha, or the *Dalles*, or my being without a fatherland".[13] As I see it, Fliess, who harbors within him a maltreated witness, refuses to let his friend testify to traumatic circumstances—probably those related to his father's bankruptcy and to the family disaster caused by the arrest and sentencing of Josef Freud, the uncle involved in counterfeit ruble trafficking.[14] A murdered witness wants to kill the witness in

Freud who claims to offer a method of reading dreams containing the traces of trials which were never conducted. Fliess wants to keep his hold on Freud, who is not only too alive himself, but who becomes the dangerous awakener of sleeping witnesses or of those left for dead.

Freud obeys the injunction and does not publish the dream. He regrets this, admits he is sad, but he *understands* his censor. This situation brings to mind children in whom "understanding" replaces anger and a refusal to comply. This psychological understanding—highly damaging—indicates that the child has not found, or has lost, the ability to turn against the one who harms him, the one whose reaction was unsuited to the child's age, or his development, or to the situation. Such understanding is a substitute for opposition. To keep his parents' love, to keep the sky above his head and the ground beneath his feet, the child foregoes launching an appeal, refrains from showing opposition, and adopts a position that accommodates his parents.

This fictional psychoanalytic account written on the theme of the birth of psychoanalysis gives the impression that a "first Freud", the masterful interpreter of the enigmas of his childhood, is willing to let a "second Freud" gain ground—a Freud in whom an ideologue equates the personal with the universal. The first Freud resembles Oedipus, the decipherer of the Sphinx's riddle, while the second Freud resembles an endogenous Oedipus, congenitally present in the child from the start. My hypothesis is that Freud sacrificed the decipherer of riddles, the interpreter of all individual traumas—of his own childhood as well as those shared by Emma—to defend a conceptual hero who could explain everything and, in that process, erase every particular trauma.

After Fliess's refusal to have the "Big Dream" published, Freud spent a year weaving the camouflage allowing him to preserve his brilliant discoveries—without disclosing their meaning. In 1899, he wrote a text entitled "Screen Memories", as well as *The Interpretation of Dreams*, in which the specimen dream, a traumatic dream if ever there was one, became the example of a normal dream—a subterfuge which allowed him to declare that: "When [...] interpretation has been completed the dream can be recognized as a wish fulfilment".[15]

Disguising the dream about the Emma affair as a paradigmatic dream, and presenting every child as a budding Oedipus—with the conflicting impulses this implies—made it possible to hide the particular events that a witness refused to recognise, and provided an explanation to cover over the refusal of the witness to testify.

This device depends on a de-metaphorisation of the sexual. When Oedipus is considered to be an endogenous seducer, the sexual is taken literally and left out of the circulation of words. This particular concept of the sexual becomes the witness to the resolution of a crisis, "witness" designating in this case something like the plaster placed by an architect between two borders of a crack in a wall, to indicate the date of the inspection. The sexual, and particularly the ready-to-wear sexual associated with primal fantasies, would soon become an efficient storage place for unresolved catastrophes. This translation of all representational content as sexual fantasy—an irrefutable translation—can, when needed, cover over the steeping in silence of false testimony, soul murder, failings, shame, betrayal, denunciation, secrets and sexual aggression. Sexual fantasy is a blanket *ad hoc* cover-up, since it is held to be the *fons et origio* of psycho-corporeal life, when in truth it is one of the preferred means of the psyche-soma to symbolise what was left unsymbolised in previous generations, to humanise the gaps created by history in the fabric of memory.

The new theory of hysteria is like the hysteric who, through his symptom, symbolises with that which denies him. Before 1896, in his trauma theory, Freud recognised that the hysteric was dealing with the dramas of his forefathers, with their defeats, shame never overcome, and even ethical death. Like the hysteric who creates his symptom out of something nameless, out of the lack of a psychic matrix of which his parents suffered, and who through this symptom launches a call for witnesses by transposing onto *another stage*—the stage of transference—the catastrophe left unrecognised in his childhood, the theory of hysteria symbolises using the very elements that destroy it, and asks us to stand witness.

During these years when Freud was dealing with the soul murder of the co-author he had chosen, he made an essential discovery which he reported in *Fragments of an Analysis of a Case of Hysteria*: the discovery that the hysteric has the genius to replay, in renewed form, the drama that holds her captive, in a desperate attempt to give it a different outcome. The theory of hysteria is a re-edition of the drama that presided over her birth, and every analyst is asked to hear this drama as the repetition of another drama which remains hidden. Every analyst is asked to take notice that Freud declared being surprised to see the Loch Ness monster appear before him, although he always knew that the monster existed.

The endogenous dual-drive theory Freud elaborates has Fliess's approval because he can see and recognise himself in it, just as he can see himself in his system of periods and his astrological calculations. In this small space limited to the sphere of an ideological system—the equivalent of a "little old key"—Fliess is protected from the risk of coming near the place without memory, which is his foundation—this moment that he lived through without experiencing it, this event which left the witness in him for dead. Freud's dualist system is the trace left in the psychoanalytic corpus by the host of the sleeping witness. These men and women so faithfully illustrated by Fliess are displaced from the place where they originated. As far as they are concerned, nothing happened, there is nothing to see or hear, nothing to look for. Their case is heard and they turn to the stars, the gods or scientistic genetics to find the meaning of the situations in which they find themselves. Like Don Juan, they are sincere when they assert that nothing happened. When Fliess agreed with the explanation provided by Oedipus and Hamlet, and when Freud accommodated him with the concept of psychic bisexuality and later with that of dual-drive thrown into the damaged kettle of the metapsychology, the cage melted in the bird. And yet the bird—in which we see Freud as a child, as well as the "first Freud" who focused his enquiry on paternal etiology and trauma—tries to detach itself from the cage that holds him captive, like a swan that tries to free itself from the ice in which its feathers are caught, or a man who strives to free himself from voluntary servitude.

In his letter to Romain Rolland, Freud writes that the disturbance he experienced on the Acropolis often returns to haunt him since he has become unable to travel. In this text on incredulity—as he calls it in his diary—he analyses the feeling of strangeness that he experienced 30 years earlier, in 1904, on the Acropolis: a part of him was astonished to see this landscape, while the other part of him had always known that it existed. He compares this experience of disbelief to the impression of someone walking beside Loch Ness who suddenly sees the form of the famous monster and is astounded, although he had never doubted its existence. Freud advances the hypothesis that this phenomenon is related to a past situation, so unbelievable and unreal that it was unlikely to produce a sensation:

> Without for the moment particularizing as to how I have arrived at the idea, I will start from the presumption that the original factor must have been a sense of some feeling of the unbelievable and the unreal in the situation at the moment. […] And now you will no longer wonder that the recollection of this incident on the Acropolis should have troubled me so often since I myself have grown old and stand in need of forebearance and can travel no more.[16]

Freud went on to say that such events produce the feeling that reality is strange or that a part of the subject is strange to him. And he added that in these situations "we are anxious to keep something out of us".

But how does the ego exclude a part of itself? Freud answers that it does what King Boabdil, the last king of Grenada, did when he was brought the message announcing the fall of Alhama, the last fortress preventing access to Grenada, the city whose loss would mean the end of his rule: he threw the letters in the fire and killed the messenger.

The "latter Freud" launches an appeal, once again, in this 1935 text, written a year before he testified that the first Moses was killed, two years after the death of his "first witness" and Grand Vizier, Sandor Ferenczi. Thus, Freud lodges an appeal about a symptom that has been plaguing him for 30 years, and is related to Fliess. This text on disbelief, he seems to say, reveals the price he paid for believing—like Elvira, Don Juan's wife—and finding himself demolished by this undeniable reality—that he is dealing with a monster—surprised and unable to believe it, although he always knew that this monster existed.

He always knew that Fliess was one of the living-dead, yet—and this is a message he addresses to the readers of the letter to Romain Rolland and of his *Moses*—he killed the messenger announcing the catastrophe. Now, he could not reveal the event that took him by surprise, when he was unprepared, despite the fact that he had always known the truth:

> Without […] particularizing as to how I have arrived at the idea, I will start from the presumption that the original factor must have been a sense of some feeling of the unbelievable and the unreal in the situation at the moment.

What he could do was make the event part of his oeuvre, in the form of a letter to a famous man.

A few weeks before this trip taken in 1904, Fliess had written Freud a letter in which he accused him of having taken part in a theft—specifically, of having allowed Otto Weininger, through Hermann Swoboda's intervention, to use Fliess's concept of bisexuality. On the ship taking him from Trieste to Athens in 1904, Freud was once again seized with the fear that Fliess's sinister predictions aroused in him. The number of his cabin and other numbers relating to him personally seemed to indicate that the hour of his death was near. In a letter written to Carl Jung in April 1909,[17] Freud admits that Fliess haunts him.

The "first Freud" has been undermined. The genius who discovered, with Breuer, that hysterics suffer mainly from reminiscence, who stated that repression is related to a refusal of translation, that the human psyche owes its complexity and its ability to deploy all its clever tricks to the fact that the auditory, visual and graphic representations of a word play as they like with the identity of the thing and the word, an identity so closely allied with common sense—that Freud has made a compromise. The genius who was developing an art of healing psychic illness, and revolutionising psychology, who discovered that between the "pervert" and the hysteric there is a filiational relation—"perverse" father and hysterical daughter—that genius was made to keep his discovery under wraps. This first Freud, like the first Moses in *Moses and Monotheism*,[18] is replaced by a second Freud who introduces a new law governing psychic functioning, a law marked by passionate love for a being who cannot testify to what he has experienced.

The kettle of metapsychology has had a hole made in it by a seducer who is a silenced defaulting witness. The blood of the theory of hysteria recently invented by the first Freud flows out through this hole. This hemorrhage, this loss of substance in which Freud, in a note added to a January 1895 letter to Fliess, recognises the figure of melancholia,[19] is associated with the cover provided to a maltreated witness.

The catastrophic ending of Freud's relation with Fliess brought into being a new theory of hysteria, which for many future analysts was going to constitute the matrix into which they fitted their work with patients. Freud was the first to conform to this theory, and Ida Bauer, renamed Dora, was the first patient who suffered its effects when she was required to confirm the aphorism engraved on the pediment of the theoretical edifice: "The seducer is in you". She was therefore told that her comments and gestures reflected her underlying sexual impulses: in the sessions, she would constantly open and close her change purse; that she had incestuous desires, since she loved Herr K; that she was homosexual because she loved Herr K's wife. Ida Bauer was the first patient whose psyche was sacrificed on an altar built to hide the soul murder suffered by Fliess, and in earlier times by Freud's ancestors, for whom Fliess was a stand-in.

Dora's therapy, broken off after two months, can be seen in hindsight as an illustration of analyses in which the relation is broken because the analyst has adopted an ideological stand that impels him to identify in his analysand's dreams the hypotheses of his theory, chosen to cover a witness's recusal. There are also numerous occasions when the analysand breaks off the therapy after adopting in great part the analyst's preconceptions, because he has been unable to put into words what he did not know he had to say to that particular analyst. In that case, the analysand does what Freud did when he incorporated a portion of Fliess's thought, broke off with him, told him he had a psychiatric disorder and, finally free, left for Rome.

This view of the theory of hysteria follows from a revision of the theory underlying practice, from a review of transference neurosis, of which we will discuss one aspect. This aspect can be seen as a corollary to our concept of psychic matrix, the semiotic envelope in which the parent holds the child. In the case of an ideal parent—theoretical, of course—the only flaw of this semiotic envelope is the trace of death. The child moves towards this flaw and is able to enter the "unspeakable community" through the hidden door of the primal scene, the universal scene that Freud has described. But this possibility is only hypothetical. Often, the parent presents the child with a particular defect in the semiotic fabric in which he is held, and this flaw masks the universal defect. From the beginning, the child moves towards the flaws of the semiotic envelope that his parents present to him. The vicissitudes and symptoms described in connection with the Oedipus complex can be seen as the effects of these defects on the parent–child relationship.

The same thing applies to transference. With the analyst's help, the patient attempts to shed the dead weight holding him down, but in the course of this long journey he gets to know his analyst so well that he immediately finds himself turning like a magnetic needle towards the deaf zones that a trauma of some kind has created in the latter's ability to listen. The analysand, who as a child had to deal with a defaulting witness, and who was the victim of soul murder, always finds himself led towards the little door behind which the analyst keeps the parts of himself left for dead. Such an analysis can only be completed if the analyst is willing to recognise a trauma towards which the analysand is led blindly.

When asked the question: "What is a psychoanalyst?", we answer that it is the person who is ready to be summoned and asked to recognise a trauma, some part of the real that a particular analysand, "because it is him, because it is her", is led to reveal.

Like a clock that has lost its counterweight, the time of psychoanalysis stopped with the death of Ferenczi, the first independent witness to the beginnings of the history of the psychoanalytic movement. Ferenczi had been Freud's pupil—not to venture to say analysand—starting in 1910, as well as his friend. Ferenczi alone, among all the disciples, was able to show himself to be on equal footing with the master, able to face him, to be at once with him and against him, *ad-versum*—a true adversary.

Four years after the death of his Grand Vizier, in 1933, Freud went back to the ongoing argument between them in the last years of their intense collaboration. In truth, this argument had been interrupted three years before Ferenczi's death. It had been related to Freud's refusal to rethink the *primum movens*, the first driving element of the psyche-soma, and to re-examine the question of the traumatic, as Ferenczi was asking him to do. But Freud flatly refused. By refusing to question the place of the sexual in his theoretical edifice, Freud was denying Ferenczi the opportunity to contribute to the foundation of psychoanalysis, and was dampening his enthusiasm.

In his work, Ferenczi was developing ideas that led to concluding, both in agreement with Freud and in disagreement with him, that the ground of the sexual was the traumatic. "With" Freud because he had opened this path in *Beyond the Pleasure Principle*, but also "against" Freud, because in his last texts, such as the *Moses* and *Analysis Terminable and Interminable*, he kept repeating that the traumatic originates in the sexual, meaning that it comes down to the difference between the sexes and to the nature of the libido.

> We often have the impression that with the wish for a penis and the masculine protest we have penetrated through all the psychological strata and have reached bedrock [...]. This is probably true, since for the psychical field, the biological field does in fact play the part of the underlying bedrock. The repudiation of femininity can be nothing else than a biological fact, a part of the great riddle of sex.[20]

If Ferenczi had read the last paragraph of this 1937 text, he could have written to the man to whom he owed so much, the man he had admired and loved for so long, that he must rethink his position. He would have said: "No, it cannot be so". And he would have shown Freud, before asking us to stand witness, that "femininity" is not a substance and that it is not possible to say that "the repudiation of femininity" is the "bedrock" on which the psyche-soma is grounded. He would have asked Freud to imagine a person who survived soul murder by splitting himself into a child still alive but asleep, like Sleeping Beauty, and a sentry who keeps close watch over this child he used to be, but who now is entrusted to him. Ferenczi would have added that this sentry guards carefully all the passages leading to the place where the child lies sleeping, so as to prevent any intrusion. To conclude, Ferenczi would have pointed out that it is not relevant to see a "repudiation of femininity" in a person protecting himself from the bodily memory of psychic annihilation.

Freud saw the fierce vigilance of the survivor of soul murder simply as a refusal of passivity, a refusal to be penetrated. For Freud to be able to accept that one "bedrock" can hide another, the sentry protecting the integrity of his corpus of work would have had to let down his guard. For this to happen, Freud would have had to agree to conduct a "mutual analysis" with Ferenczi, and would have had to finally admit that he was inhabited by a wounded being, a Fliess who held such an important place in the Freudian corpus, particularly in this text—one of his later writings. Then, he could have admitted that a person who survives soul murder is grounded in a particular "primal scene", an originary scene that has replaced the universally assumed primal scene.

Had this taken place, Freud would have been able to sustain the vital tension between the universal and the particular, between the pathological and the normal, between psychosis and neurosis, between denial and repression. As a result, the pathological would not have been submerged by a flood of the normal.

Notes

1 Freud, S., *The Complete Letters of Sigmund Freud to Wilhelm Fliess, 1887–1904*, Masson, J.M. (Ed.), Cambridge, MA, Harvard University Press, 1985, p. 207.

2 Historians and sociologists have invented the term "negationist" to designate those who deny the Nazi policy of extermination of the Jews. I believe that among these there are some people who have tricked death, who have been subjected to the murder of the witness in themselves.

3 "*Man findet in Traum das Kind weiterlebendmitseinenImpulsen*" (Freud, S., "Die Traumdeutung", *in Studienausgabe, Bd II*, Berlin, Fischer Verlag, 1972, p. 203).

4 Why Freud broke off with Breuer to have such an exclusive relationship with Fliess is an interesting question. For a long time, Fliess appeared as a substitute for Jakob Freud, the *Luftmensch* who roamed the streets of Vienna just as Monsieur Joyeuse—Alphonse Daudet's character mentioned in *The Interpretation of Dreams*—does in Paris to make his daughters believe that he still has an office and a job. I saw in Fliess an image of Jakob Freud although, on the surface, they were complete opposites, since one went bankrupt and remained a failure, while the other encountered exceptional success. In effect, both are broken men; one pretends nothing happened, while the other is utterly unable to say what happened. Despite the convenience of this sharp yet almost invisible resemblance, I don't think this was the main factor responsible for bringing about the "only passion that Freud ever lived", as Ernest Jones described this friendship. To think that Freud transferred onto Fliess the feelings he had had for his father—an idea inherent to my hypothesis—does not explain the reciprocal passion felt by Fliess for Freud. Another shortcoming of this explanation is that it is an element of the foundation Freud built after his theoretical edifice was exposed to possible collapse once trauma theory was set aside.

5 The secret of his miraculous therapy could be summed up in this magic formula: "A *Muschel* (muscle) is a *Muschel* (*mussle*)", where the first refers to the nasalis muscle, the scientific designation of a part of the anatomy of the nose, and the second refers to the female genitals in French street language. The formula "A muscle (nasal turbinet) is a muscle (vulva)" sounds like a variant of the mechanism Freud identified in schizophrenics: "What has dictated the substitution is not the resemblance between the things denoted but the sameness of the words used [...], 'a hole [turbinet] is a hole [vagina]'" (Sigmund Freud, *The Unconscious*, S.E. 14:166–204).

6 "A cage went in search of a bird", in Kafka's *The Zürau Aphorisms*. This meditation stayed enigmatic for me for a long time, before I understood something of its meaning.

7 We are indebted to Fliess for having kept the correspondence from Freud—except the letters describing the "specimen dream"—and it is thanks to him that we have the archives containing the traces of the drama marking the turning point in their relations, and more importantly, the turning point in the evolution of psychoanalysis.

8 Freud, S., *The Complete Letters of Sigmund Freud to Wilhelm Fliess, 1887–1904*, op. cit.

9 "The value of [Freud's] method is that it provides anyone who knows the psyche with a new and very refined instrument—but very fragile—for exploring the unconscious. However, it is of no use at all to bunglers of souls" (Max Graf, father of Little Hans, quoted in Sylwan, B., and Réfabert, P., *Freud, Fliess, Ferenczi. Des fantômes qui hantent la psychanalyse, Paris, Hermann, 2010*, p. 95.)

10 As to what became of the other two people who signed this birth certificate, it appears that Wilhelm Fliess never went beyond the closed sphere where his ideas were circumscribed; Emma Eckstein, after a brief period of a few years when she became a practising psychoanalyst, retired to her couch and remained a partial invalid, suffering from astasis or abasia. If Freud would have understood that she was letting him know that "it can't work this way", psychoanalysis would have been changed.

11 The drama played out between Emma Eckstein, Freud and Fliess does not imply that her psychic suffering was created by Fliess's refusal to admit his error, and by Freud's willingness to cover this up. Emma found herself faced with a missing witness because such a scene was part of her past and she was trying to give it a different ending than it had originally, in her childhood. The fact that these therapists were unable to invent this ending was not of her doing, but she was the one attempting to recreate the scene. For this reason, she could not let Freud know about the damage inflicted on her except in a message appearing to be a screen, but which could also be interpreted as a call for witnesses.

12 Sylwan, B. and Réfabert, P., *Freud, Fliess, Ferenczi*, op. cit., p. 290. Barbro Sylwan discovered that the critic using the pen name Ry was probably doctor Rischavy, and that a doctor by this name was related to Freud. The brother-in-law of Freud's eldest daughter Mathilde was, in fact, a doctor Rischavy. Mathilde's married name was Holitscher and her husband's sister was married to a doctor Rischavy who could have been the author of the diatribe which condemned Fliess with such astounding determination. Barbro Sylwan supposed that Freud's family and close friends could have been irritated by the exclusive and passionate nature of a collaboration which, in their eyes, had gone on too long. She felt that the merciless character of the judgment which excluded Fliess and his research from the scientific community could have been an expression of this exasperation.

13 Freud, S., *The Complete Letters of Sigmund Freud to Wilhelm Fliess*, op. cit.

14 I have tried to reconstruct this dream and the letter in which Freud described it to his friend—a letter he exceptionally asked Fliess to return to him, no doubt so that he could burn it. To write the letter, I drew on "Screen Memories", a text Freud wrote during the period of listless depression in which Fliess's prohibition of the dream had plunged him. Not only was the letter recounting the dream censured by Fliess, but also by the "editors" of the Freud–Fliess correspondence in 1950, who erased all traces of it almost completely: Réfabert, P., "*Colloque de Chiens* (2) The Letter in which Freud Reveals His Big Dream to Fliess", *Temps Modernes*, No. 613, 2001.

15 Freud, S. (1900), *The Interpretation of Dreams*, S.E. 4–5, London: Hogarth.

16 Freud, S., *A Disturbance of Memory on the Acropolis*, S.E. 22, London: Hogarth.

17 Freud, S. and Jung, C., *The Freud/Jung Letters*, Berkley, CA, Princeton University Press, 1994.

18 Freud, S., *Moses and Monotheism*, New York, Vintage Books, 1955. This book is a testament of sorts, written between 1936 and 1938.

19 Freud, S., *The Complete Letters of Sigmund Freud to Wilhelm Fliess*, op. cit.

20 Freud, S., *Analysis Terminable and Interminable*, S.E. 23, London: Hogarth, p. 252.

9

The Witness

Subject of Psychoanalysis

Here, I propose that we look at psychoanalysis from the perspective of witnessing. This point of view occurred to me when I reconsidered the concept of "soul murder" that Judge Schreber borrowed from German literature. It seems to me that this perspective should be extended to the entire range of psychopatologies, and that it would be beneficial to view psychotherapy as an experience where the analyst creates conditions allowing the witness in the analysand to feel that his ability to testify has been restored, if not outright reconstituted.

Freud strove all his life to make his metapsychology consistent. Throughout the duration of his research he re-examined its basic concepts and, at the age of 65, he proposed a conceptual tool—repetition compulsion at work "beyond the pleasure principle"—which would change clinical perspective and analytic listening. But the theoretical revision that this new idea announced did not come to pass, and Freud's concept remained hampered by ontological sequestra[1] incompatible with the dynamics it promoted. As all founders of a new scientific field do, Freud grounded his thought in the knowledge of his century, and his reasoning necessarily harboured accepted principles[2] opposed to the revolutionary ideas he had introduced.

Freud's death and the institutionalisation of psychoanalysis contributed for years afterwards to reinforce the conservative trends which restricted psychoanalytic thought to a dogmatic corpus. Yet research stayed alive, even though the psychoanalysts who conducted it were relegated to the margins of the field, or completely ostracised. What was needed was to widen the field of application of "talk therapy", to reestablish the borderline between neurosis and psychosis, as Freud defined it; to eliminate the false dilemma opposing fantasy and trauma; to maketransference dynamics and the concept of origin of the subject[3] compatible.

It occurred to me that placing the *witness* at the centre of the perspective afforded by psychoanalytic theory would renew our thinking by using other words to say what has already been stated; it would also dispel certain needless difficulties. The first witness—the mother—is the one who testifies to the discontinuity of human existence by creating a counterinvestment in the face of the void. I have suggested that we see this originary closing off, this initial gift, as a specific maternal donation. "Primal repression" is the consequence of an opposition to the limitless, to

DOI: 10.4324/9781003435730-11

extinction. The creation of the *subject* is the dazzling moment when the I takes possession of the break in the limitless, a break allowing the I to see its image, the Ego. In this process, the negative becomes connected to the positive, the *no* inherent to existence is inscribed in the *yes* inherent to essence, [4] to allow the emergence of a subject, this paradoxical entity constituted of the indissociable alliance of the "same" and the "other", of "yes" and of "no".

The dazzling moment of the creation of the subject that I am occurs when the I separates from the other person (the mother), who instantly becomes other than me. Until then, this other held the place of the "I" and looked at "me". This idea was put into words by Nicolas Abraham, who spoke of a "crime of introjection".

The subject gains his independence through the separation between an interiorised "other" and an "other" henceforth external. The interiorised other acts as a witness for the child.

Freud conceived of "primal repression"—that he saw as a counterinvestment—in order to confer coherence to the concept of the unconscious he was elaborating. This is how he came to grant the child, on principle, the capacity for reflection associated with the inscription of the other in the same. In his haste to establish the foundation of the new field he was delimiting, Freud assumed that the essential question of the creation of the subject had been resolved. Since that time, all analysts who have contributed to the development of psychoanalysis have felt the need to re-examine this question. "Primal repression", this counterinvestment of the void, this objection, this "no" put forth to hold back the void, depends on the conditions the child encounters at birth. This repression is never perfect, and the child will always have to deal with a *nameless thing* which tends to cover over the trace of death—this unknowable *thing* nevertheless recognised by the human community and surrounded by rituals.

Each time a child is brought into the word, the parent passes on a part of the world under cover, outside the laws of language. This clandestine part of the world has no existence; it cannot be represented; its shadowless presence demands attention; it *is*there, but does not exist. Hence, it cannot disappear. It insists, and the child who ventures to explore and identify the things constituting the world is inexorably attracted by it. He can't ignore it.

A fact can only enter the sphere of reality when it has acquired completion, when it has been assigned a negative value that draws it out of the limitless. Something that was not recognised by the parent is, at it were, evacuated with the delivery of the child. The child deals with a nameless thing, instead of dealing with the trace of death; he accommodates this unnamed—unnamable thing and his primal fantasies are based on it.

Freud formulated a universal law when he suggested that the child's fantasies are elaborated based on the "primal scene", this blank zone that impossible representation carves out in the psyche. But such a universal law supposes a theoretical mother and father—that is, abstract—symbolic, in the Lacanian sense. Such transcendental parents, however, in possession of their own death, as Rilke says, whose only ambition is the peaceful succession of generations, do not exist in reality. The child will always create his original fantasies using the traces of some nameless thing, and will put together his own "primal scene".

The entire metapsychology must be restructured when its cornerstone is no longer made upof ready-made primal fantasies and, presumably, a universal "primal scene", which finds as many applications as Euclidian geometry finds in nature.

The quality of a parent lies in his ability to let himself be questioned by the child seeking a nameless thing which exerts a powerful attraction. When the mother heeds the suggestion—in her thoughts or in her dreams—that she is responsible for everything that happens to the child, she allows the child to demand that she examine a left-out part of herself. The parent's ethics depend on his willingness to look for blocked-out facts masking the nameless thing evacuated at the birth of the child, outside of language and unbeknownst to the parent. When the child is faced with gaps created on the run in the envelope enclosing him, he senses the rhythmic inadequacies they create in the mother's holding. The child reacts by screaming, crying, and eventually by developing a symptom. When there is no response, the child's fate depends on the ability of the other parent to offer a different response than that of the mother. This *witnessing* roleis an important component of the paternal function.

When the father refuses to play this role, he leaves it to the child to avoid, on his own, the void towards which the nameless thing draws him. This child is then placed in a situation where "there is nothing of time and space", to quote Hölderlin speaking of Oedipus's despair when all representation was abolished with the destruction of his world. When the witness is eliminated, the *subject* loses footing and "primal repression" is reconstituted extemporaneously at the expense of the Ego; in other words, the child, in a flash—a lightning flash associated with all acts of creation—brings into being a *new subject*, a *prophetic subject*. He accomplishes this rescue operation by negating a part of himself, with which he replaces the missing negation, to instantly invent a new "primal repression".[5]

All forms of psychopathology deserve to be described in light of this withdrawal of the witness, or of his betrayal. Often, the child's suffering is due to his status of hostage of parents who seem to have made an unconscious pact entrusting one another with safeguarding the other's repression. They act as if each of them was the guardian of a closet in which the other keeps, at random, all things in the world for which he takes no responsibility. When fortuitous events risk coming too close to these things, one of the parents, covered by the other, places the child in a state of privation, with no awareness whatever of his responsibility.

I trade you my secret for yours. Give-and-take. You say nothing about the Eskimo woman and I say nothing about the Jewish woman. This was the situation faced by Henry, who had an attack of herpes after every visit to his parents. This child's parents had both focused a sharp gaze on him. One detected in his features the traits of an Eskimo woman with whom a great-grandfather had had a child, before using his privileges as a coloniser to take it away from her. The other parent saw the son as resembling a very rich Jewish woman whom a grandfather had married to improve his social standing. The two secrets focused on the same object, in this case Henry.

The story of the game of hide-and-seek in which parents suddenly hide from a very young child, and then reappear as saviours after letting him suffer a panic attack, is a perfect illustration of the moment of absolute privation which can found the existence of certain analysands. This diabolical scene reminds me of a story in the Talmud about a pregnant woman who was attacked by a dog unexpectedly and felt her child instantly detach himself in her womb. Her host's assurances that he had taken care to pull out the dog's teeth and remove his claws are of no use, she tells him, since she clearly felt the baby detach itself. This woman and the child subjected to the game of hide-and-seek are in a similar situation: their respective aggressors want to believe that what they are doing is harmless. In the first case the foetus dies, detached from the womb; in the second case, the child is alive but the witness in him who allowed him to associate his symptom to its cause has been killed or is completely stupefied. In order to keep his parents, the child pretends that he has not lost them.

When the parents forfeit their role as witnesses by becoming aggressors, the child's internal witness, the I, goes into hibernation. This witness who always stood next to him until then, just as Humphrey Bogart's ghost is a constant invisible presence next to Woody Allen in *Play It Again, Sam*, this witness the child had introjected, had made his own, has now been plunged into deep sleep. Sometimes the witness dies, as is the case in paranoia. Here, the other in the child, the witness, has been killed and instantly replaced by a double of the subject. In this situation, the subject does not have a place from which to see himself, since he perceives the world through a cloned system "I–I" or "me–me", instead of "I–me". But, in most cases, the witness is plunged into a comatose state, like Snow White.

When the child is faced with the joint refusal of his parents to turn back on themselves and assume their part of responsibility for what he experiences, the child swallows his pain and saves what he can by becoming a *new subject*, a *prophetic subject*. This child, after trying to show his suffering—through screams, fits of anger, crying, symptoms—gives up in a flash and acts *as if* he felt nothing. He finds himself de-tested—deprived of a witness—deprived of that for which the parent can't take responsibility, and he confirms a situation he sees as natural. This child, elevated onto the high plateau of tombless souls, innocently sings to his parent the tune of "the wilderness of the dead" (Hölderlin). He has become a Sphynx-child who asks enigmatic questions, like the singing dog. The parent does not understand this song and is soon so irritated by it that he takes "disciplinary measures". But one day, the child, tired of crying and being angry, lays down his arms, gives up his anger and instantly constitutes himself into a prophetic subject.

By doing this, the child saves his tutelary powers from the danger to which he senses them to be exposed and, above all, preserves his link with the originary witnesses who set the foundations of the perceptions Aristotle called the "common sensibles".[6] This child shares with the philosopher the certainty that "if a man sees a tree and needs proof of it, it is a sign of serious illness". To "save what you can" means to retreat before danger—a risk taken by delinquents—to leave the communality of sensing—this sensing together—that the child shares with his parents. To save this communality, to keep the sense and evidence of a common perception, he forfeits his pain before inventing, as an alternate form of conservation, an adequate translation, a symptom.

The analyst keeps in mind the intention of the analysand to return to the catastrophic moment when he *changed into another subject*. If the analyst himself has experienced this psychotic extremity, as Winnicott says, if he has stopped paying back a debt he had not incurred, if he has put down the baggage he was carrying for others, if he has been able to say "no" to cut-out events in the world for which he had accepted responsibility, then he can claim to stand witness.

His ethical position is established by the means he gives himself to reanimate the witness in the analysand, a fragile witness, ready to give up the fight and fade out of view once again. The analyst knows that all he can do is to create the most favourable conditions for the crossing during which the prophetic subject, constructed in the urgency of survival, will face the counter-rhythmic caesura described by Hölderlin, in this "pure speech" which—on the mode of that of Tiresias in *Oedipus the King* and in *Antigone*—makes it impossible to maintain the old balance. The analyst willing to withstand the crisis which will render the prophetic subject disloyal to himself respects the fact that it is the analysand who conducts the analysis, and who decides when he will take the leap, leaving behind the habits and symptoms he had invented to "resist" as Celan says.

I think it essential to start by awakening this witness, that is, uncovering, with the analysand, how his family and the circle in which he lives have dealt with the gaps in the history of his lineage, and what rhetorical contortions they have had to invent to cover over these gaps; how communication was perturbed when the ethical obligation to testify was cast aside, scorned, sacrificed to the ideology[7] of a parent, a family member, a social group or the nation.[8]

As a child, Chris was often told that he had a poor memory, that he wasn't good at memorising things. At the dinner table, his father would hold up household objects and ask him to name them. This family had a secret that kept everyone silent. It had to do with a grandfather who did some ill-advised business, behaved badly and was said not to have all his marbles. Chris was tacitly considered to take after him, and these educational exercises were supposed to compensate for his deficiency.

By distortions, I mean errors in destination reinforced by habit, which lead the child to play the role of therapist, and even "parent", with his parents, when the latter have not done the work being carried out now by the analysand—work which consists of taking possession of one's own origins as a subject. Recognising the monstrous nature of such an inversion allows the analysand to regain access to an unclaimed sensation, for instance, to connect a feeling of exhaustion with a visit to his parents.

From my place as a witness, I assist the analysand on the journey that leads him, *nolensvolens*, to admit the fact that a parent strove to cover up the soul murder perpetrated against him, and that he still appeals to his child to confirm the "forgetting" he has constructed. At the same time, this parent also asks the child to be the witness he never had. And the child becomes used to answering these contradictory demands, despite the harm inflicted on him each time he plays this expected role. If he refuses, he is accused of not respecting his parent. "But she is your mother", Carrot Top's father tells him when he defies his mother's wishes. The parent who does not know that he suffered psychic agony cannot take the bad upon himself. He automatically tends to distort all time and space parameters that define the respective positions held by parent and child. I have sometimes shown that such a parent behaves as if time was reversible, does not assert the fact that he brought the child into the world, and speaks and acts as if his child was a brother, a sister, or a parent. It is as if death does not exist for this parent, because it has already occurred, and the child finds himself without anyone to *attest* to his origin. This child must bring proof that soul murder has not taken place. He does so through his success at school, his "*joie de vivre*" and his excellent health. He must also tolerate his parents' invasiveness, as well as its justification. Sometimes, the parent not only invades the child's privacy, but doubles his helplessness by blaming himself and pretending to make up for it by providing psychological—even "psychoanalytical"—explanations concerning his own childhood.

The patching up of the symbolic content of discourse offers the analysand the possibility of revisiting the catastrophe that caused him to crystallise into a prophetic subject. The analyst disposes the "soul" of the analysand, the witness in him, to come out of his stupefaction. But this mending is only a prelude, and what counts is what happens between the analyst and the analysand, because a prophetic subject cannot risk losing his frame of reference without the concrete reassurance he can only find in his lived experience with the analyst, in the transference. What I mean is that he must feel that the analyst has paid or is paying with his own person, before abandoning the crutch for which he paid so dearly but which provided some kind of support.

The one who was betrayed by a *Nebenmensch*, or worse, saw him turn angrily against him and become his aggressor, is a subject who has only one paradoxical way to effect a change. Blindly and unconsciously he creates the conditions that will reproduce the injury he suffered, in case the aggressor might reconsider his aggression, admit to it and thus become a witness. The one who has lost his anger, who learned to ignore his sensations and his pain, who can no longer make a request, cannot avoid prompting another person to *repeat the crime against him* that was left unprosecuted. This is enacted in analysis.

The analyst was led to feel hatred towards Carmela, and it was only by recognising this feeling that he narrowly avoided repeating the crime committed against her. For several weeks, during her twice-weekly sessions, Carmela sat facing the analyst, sullen and silent, rejecting all of his interventions and invitations to speak. Everything he said was disputed or ridiculed. The analyst felt like sending her to the devil and in session after session he tried as best he could to fight this very unpleasant and inadmissible feeling. For two weeks he tried to identify what exactly created this feeling in him. Until the day he was able to tell her—and this was very frightening—that she made him feel hatred towards her. To his great surprise, Carmela's face lit up and she smiled as she had not done in a long time. "Finally, someone dares to tell me. I notice that people feel this way about me everywhere I go". In this session, the analyst had made her the gift—for which he had paid the price—of being able to name a feeling which was excluded from her parents' universe. Later, when she questioned family members, she learned that she had been fed through a funnel after the birth of a little sister, until late in her childhood.

"The crime is always repeated". When Ferenczi stated this law, at the end of his life, I think he was referring to analysands who have lost the ability to turn against a parent because they realised—almost inevitably—that the parent and his tutelary power have been diverted from them. When their analyst blunders or makes a mistake, they have accidents, are late for their session, have a herpes flare-up, or else retreat into silence or even a "depression". Rather than point out an error of judgment to their analyst, rather than confront him, they defend themselves through a "transference" symptom, just as they had done in their childhood when they created a symptom.

In his work with Louise, encouraged by the friendly collaboration reigning in the sessions, the analyst had extended his comprehension and sympathy to an older sister involved in his patient's upbringing. In fact, this sister constantly humiliated Louise on the pretext of giving her an education. In the next session, when she told him that after the previous session she had hurt herself badly when she hitherself hard against her car door, the analyst attributed this accident to his betrayal. When he expressed concern and understanding of the tormenting sister, he repeated the injury. When he connected the accident with the session, he acknowledged both the present-day "crime" and the past crime.

Charles, who was very sensitive to the quality of the analyst's presence, had spent his childhood with an unavailable mother, busy playing solitaire in her own world. He himself had inherited this obsession, of which he had recently been able to free himself. In a session, the analyst heard Charles' speech peter out little by little. After a long silence, he made the embarrassing admission that he had been playing solitaire. The analyst was able to answer that by not giving him his full attention, by taking up his appointment book, he had not been present to Charles and had thus repeated the crime he suffered as a child.

One day, the analyst found Edith on the landing in front of his office, where she had been coming for years. "Excuse me", she said, "I got here early". In truth, the analyst had forgotten this appointment and was very late, contrary to his habit. Another day, the analyst was very surprised by the trite and empty character of Edith's discourse, which was unlike her; he realised that this was a discreet sign on her part, her way of reacting to the somewhat brutal tone he had employed in the previous session. He was able to bring to light, with her help, the fact that at the age of one she had been left alone in her crib for a longer time than was reasonable.

The analysand, like the child, comes to curl up—under the influence of transference—in front of the secret door the analyst does not know that he keeps closed. And the analysand knocks on this door, behind which the analyst keeps the unthought thing on which he has constructed himself. The worst happens when the analyst—like the parent earlier—is unaware of the knock, feels no discomfort or anxiety, or strives to ignore them.

Notes

1 In the medical sense of the word, the sequestrum is "a necrotic fragment of bone which separates from the rest of the living bone".

2 For instance, Broussais' principle, stating that the difference between the normal and the pathological is only a matter of degree. Freud insisted on this law, without stating it explicitly.

3 Freud presumed the creation of the subject to be a given. Through the concept of instinct, defined in relation to the inside of the body, which is defined relative to instinct, Freud was granting the subject the ability to "judge what is good and bad for him". Winnicott's work takes up Freud's entire theoretical construction and reformulates it. Whereas Freud assumed this problem to have been solved, Winnicott re-examined the foundations and, by doing so, made subject theory compatible with transference.

4 Rosenzweig, F., *The Star of Redemption*, Notre Dame, IN, University of Notre Dame Press, 1985.

5 Réfabert, P., *From Freud to Kafka*, London, Karnac, 2014.

6 According to Aristotle, the common sensibles are the foundation of our reasoning. The categories under this designation include "rest", "movement", "number", etc., on which we base our impression of the obvious. Loraux, P., "Consentir", *Le Genre Humain*, no. 22, 1990.

7 I am borrowing Hannah Arendt' definition: "Ideological thinking orders facts into an absolutely logical procedure which starts from an axiomatically accepted premise, deducing everything else from it; [...] it proceeds with a consistency that exists nowhere in the realm of reality". Arendt, H., *The Origins of Totalitarianism*, Cleveland, The World Publishing Company, 1951, p. 471.

8 In their works, Ferenczi, Abraham, Torok, Pankow and Lacan all confirm the impressive pathogenic power exerted by these defaulting witnesses who keep silent—because "life must go on"—and who overlook the principle of the aid that must be brought to souls abandoned by the wayside. There was no justice for these souls in the haste to forget the private consequences of the collective madness which in our part of the world took the form of colonisation, the Dreyfus affair, the Great War of 1914–1918, Vichy. The unthinkable reached its acme in what Paul Celan refused to designate otherwise than by the syntagm "that which happened" (*Was geshah*). In his book *L'Histoire confisquée de la destruction des Juifs d'Europe. Usages d'unetragédie* (Paris, Presses universitaires de France, 2016), Georges Bensoussan gives us a remarkable and quasi-exhaustive analysis of the forces which tend to erase "'that which happened'" by associating it with the thinkable. One way to do this is to classify it as a war crime, but the most subtle method is, paradoxically, to submit the unthinkable to dutiful commemoration.

10

In the Crevice of Time

Was geschah? What happened?
The stone stepped from the mountain. /
Who woke up? You and I /
Language. Language. Co-star. By earth. /
Poorer. Open. At home.[1]

Why Celan? Because he writes after what happened. It is why I need to start from Celan, after having written starting from Kafka, because, as Jean-François Lyotard says in a pivotal little book entitled *Heidegger and "the Jews"*: "Celan 'after' Kafka, Joyce 'after' Proust, Nono 'after' Mahler, Beckett 'after' Brecht, Rothko and Barnett Newman 'after' Matisse.[2]

And in Primo Levi's words:

We the survivors are not the true witnesses. […] Those who [touched bottom], those who saw the Gorgon, have not returned to tell about it or have returned mute, but they are the "Muslims", the submerged, the complete witnesses, the ones whose deposition would have a general significance.[3]

The drowned are those whose souls expired before they died in the flesh, those whose death was stolen from them, whose subjectivity was destroyed. It is in order to let such a one speak that Celan speaks: to place his ability to name and his poetic genius at his service, as if he was saying: "I remember your memories" to the one whose lips can mouth nothing.

Entmündigte Lippe... —Disenfranchised lip, announce/that something happens, still, /not far from you.[4]

In owlflight, near/ petrified leprosy, / near/ our fled hands, in/ the latest fault lines [*der jüngstenVerwerfung*].[5]

What happened? No less than the destruction of sense when the most cultured nation in the world, homeland of great philosophers and musicians, unexpectedly abolished the accomplishment of modernity—the possibility of granting sense to all speaking beings. When this nation reinstated the founding principle of primitive peoples, that is: "We are the true men", and proceeded to decide who is, or is not, part of "humanity", it established "the latest fault lines" and carried out the ultimate rejection (*der jüngsten Verwerfung*). Nothing happened when that nation, under cover of war, undertook a purification project by eliminating "parasites", after the

DOI: 10.4324/9781003435730-12

insane. Nothing happened that could explain that a people—in this case the Jews—were excluded from "humanity". Not within the realm of sense.

You can't ask "why". There is no room for a question like Primo Levi's, when he tries to quench his thirst with an icicle hanging from a roof. There is no place for the question of the one who was the object of the ultimate rejection. There is no longer room for "the" question, the one which, according to a medieval commentary, was given as a divine gift to the Israelites in the desert: *man hou*, translated as "manna", and which, the same midrash tells us, can also mean "What is it?" The question asks what nourishes the *infans*.

"What happened? The stone stepped from the mountain/Who awakened? You and I./Language. Language. Fellow-star. Earth-cousin./Poorer. Open. Homeland-like". What happened makes no more sense than the fact that a stone separates from the mountain. We are awakened by the question. Who exactly, "we"? You and I, we awaken each other. There is language and language. The language of "he" and neutral language, only this and the language of I and of you. There is the sky and the earth, but not apart, connected. Poorer. Language has become poorer, but open, questioning. And "homeland-like", like being home... with a shadow. What happened? Nothing... Only a radical change of direction on the uninterrupted path of change.

The speech register that brings about change in the very essence of the essential, a change which is not an addition to the given, is the register of the "it", Celan believes. Linguist Emile Benveniste designates this neutral form of language, that of the "it", as a non-person fraudulently called "third".[6] The language of "he", that French philosopher Fabrice Midal calls our golden calf, was that of the philosophers until not long ago; this very old language is that of an unalterable present emanating from a being outside of time who is the supposed guarantor of truth, power and the I. This language of the concept which erases the unthinkable originary anguish and abolishes discontinuity eliminates the need for the immemorial. This language sees horror being historicised, sees the real—unrepresented and unrepresentable—occasioning representation and plastified recollection.

> Black milk of morning we drink
>   you evenings
> we drink you at noon and mornings
>   we drink you at night
> we drink and we drink
> [...]
> we dig a grave in the air there one
>   lies at ease.
>
> A man lives in the house he plays with
>   snakes he writes
> he writes when it darkens to Deutschland
>   your golden hair Margarete
> he writes and steps in front of his house
> and the stars glisten and he whistles his
>   dogs to come

he whistles his jews to appear let a grave
        be dug in the earth
he commands us play up the dance.
Black milk of dawn we drink you at night
we drink you mornings and noontime
        we drink you evenings
we drink and we drink.[7]

In 1948, Celan published "Death Fugue". The poem became famous and brought him recognition and fame. The unanimous public interest the poem aroused soon turned it into a tool for reconciliation based on *Verwerfung*, the rejection of what took place. The same thing happened with the account written by Anne Frank, the little princess with almond-shaped eyes, which was misused in those years. In Hamburg, her memory was celebrated every year and became the allegory of the German people's suffering under the bombardments. Reconciliation based on rejection and deflection met with opposition from Celan and later from Jean Améry, an author Celan no doubt read as soon as his essays were published.

The poet admits that he betrayed himself by writing his fugue in the old tradition of poetry since Aristotle, which portrays reality. He understands that by respecting the rationale of poetry since ancient times, mimesis, the imitation of nature through a "swirl of metaphors", he went astray. He writes to his wife that in his first collection of poems he still used transfiguration, but that he would never do it again.

> That which is perceived and to be perceived one time, one time over and over again, and only now and only here. And the poem would then be the place where all tropes and metaphors are developed ad absurdum.[8]

The reception his poem received taught Celan that the representation of the real, its historicisation, produces a redoubling of rejection.

> Whoever is prepared only to mourn for the almond-eyed beauty [Anne Frank], kills her too [...] another time [and] buries her deeper into forgetting.[9]

Historicisation succeeds in allowing what happened to pass. After all, everything passes. Or "one gets over it". Representation of the real redoubles the rejection occurring in time's crevasse.

> Whoever [among victims of the Nazis] lazily and cheaply forgives, subjugates himself to the social and biological time-sense [...] Man has the right and the privilege to declare himself to be in disagreement with every natural occurrence, including the biological healing that time brings about. What happened happened. This sentence is just as true as it is hostile to morals and intellect.[10]

> Eroded by/the beamwind of your speech/the gaudy chatter of the pseudo-/
> experienced—the hundred-/tongue perjury-/poem, the noem
> [...]
> Deep/in the timecrevasse/ in the/honeycomb-ice/ waits, a breath crystal, / your unalterable/testimony.[11]

The collective symptom Celan encounters resembles, all things being equal, the split observed in our clinical work in a person cut off from the catastrophe on which he has built himself as a subject, who lives his life as if nothing happened. Displaced from the juncture between I and Thou, the Thou he once was, he is condemned to live in the light, deprived of the shadow where his Thou lies, his Self, as Winnicott would say.

> Speak, you too,
> speak last,
> have your say.
> Speak—
> But do not split the No from the Yes.
> Give your saying also meaning:
> give it its shadow.
> [...]

Look around:

> see how it all comes alive—
> At death! Alive!
> Speaks true, who speaks shadows.[12]

Restoring the connection between I and Thou, what Celan calls the encounter, occurs at the end of a process he designates as the poem, and we designate as analysis. In this process, a point of reversal is constituted by a counter-word, pronounced by Lucile.

Lucile, a character in Büchner's *Danton's Death*,[13] breaks the thread of the language of "he", the flow of discourses, impersonal and rhetorical, pronounced by Danton and his friends at the foot of the scaffold they are about to mount to be beheaded. Lucile is the one:

> who hears and listens and looks... and then doesn't know what the talk was all about. But who hears the speaker, "sees him speak", who perceives language and shape, and also [...] breath, that is, direction and destiny.[14]

"Long live the King!" she shouts at the foot of the scaffold where her husband and her friends mounted before her. Celan says *Gegenwort*, counter-word. Lucile doesn't know artful, artificial language, she doesn't understand grand speeches. She speaks the words of an I: "Long live the King"; counter-word, a break with consensus.

> Here, homage is being paid to the majesty of the absurd (through this dissonant scream) as witness for the presence of the human.[15]

The majesty which bears witness to human presence, but also to the Thou, the submerged—is a dissonance. It reminds split normopaths of their Thou, it addresses believers, issues a *fatwa*, signifies a rejection (*Verwerfung*) to the proponents of to-day's religion, that of progress, reminding them that light implies shadow.

Celan speaks for you, you the submerged. In his alphabet book, Deleuze speaks for animals, while Faulkner speaks for the simple-minded—and he is dissonant, he has the majesty of dissonance. The speech of such a subject is jarring. It disturbs "the bourgeoisie reconciled with a world whose shock waves it had undeniably felt".[16]

The counter-word is not unlike the axe Kafka refers to in a letter to his friend Oscar Pollak:

> If the book we're reading doesn't wake us up with a blow to the head, what are we reading for? [...] A book must be the axe for the frozen sea within us.[17]

The same is true of an analysis. Adorno, who wrote about Schoenberg's music and about his rejection of "harmonies that accompanied horror", understood at once that Celan, like Beckett, acknowledged "time's crevasse" in his work by signifying it, since he could not represent it. In analysis, the counter-word marks a significant event: it restores a part of the Thou that was rejected. It sounds dissonant to an external listener. It emerges in the course of an ongoing analysis. For instance, I once heard myself say in a session: "Your mother had no children". Similarly, Winnicott told an analysand: "I am listening to a girl".

> These dates and moments, they cannot be read off the calendars and clocks, the "old war-horses and bystanders of history" miss them; only the victims of what appears from the perspective of that "bystander" as history, know something about it.[18]

The poem emerges in the reversal that initiates the process of filling the gap between the I and the Thou, a Thou that cannot be abandoned. On this condition, the poem speaks on behalf of the Strangest-of-all, of the feeble-minded, of the submerged, of the animal.

> Ricercar...
> Your reversal—what is that? Is it the word from the almond-eyed beauty, that I hear you repeat, varied most opportunistically? Only when with your most own pain you'll have been with the crooked-nosed and yiddy and goitery dead of Auschwitz and Treblinka and elsewhere, will you also meet the eye and the almond. And then you stand with your falling silent thinking in the pause which reminds you of your heart, and don't speak of it. And speak, later, of yourself. In this "later", in there, remembered pauses, in the cola and mora, your word speaks; the poem today—it is a breathturn, crest-times and soul-turn, that's how you recognize it—be aware of it.[19]

In Celan's language, to write means "to write ourselves" in conversation with "the strangest". And his poetry acquires its meaning, for me, starting with the counter-word which points the poet in the irrevocable direction he follows in his fight against forgetting, the forgetting of the unimaginable anguish—to which we shall return later—but first of all against the forgetting of the submerged, the forgetting of the poet Mandelstam, the forgetting of Celan's mother, of the six million assassinated after their humanity was destroyed. To take the risk of writing poetry is to provide a tomb to the one who is up there, in the air: "In the air, there your root remains, there, in the air".[20] We wrote to each other and I encountered myself. "I am you when I I am".[21]

Celan's fight is waged against the forgetting of the forgetting of the unimaginable anguish, or, in metaphysical terms, against primal repression.

> Everything is different from what you think, from what I think,
> [...]
> the name Osip comes toward you, you
> tell him
> what he already knows, he takes it, he takes
> it off you with hands,
> you detach his arms from their shoulder, the
> right, the left,
> you fasten yours in their stead, with hands,
> with fingers, with lines,
> —what tore off, grows back together again—
> you have them now, so take them now,
> you have them both,
> the name, the name, the hand, the hand,
> there, take them as you pledge,
> he takes that too, and you have
> again what's yours, what was his, [22]

To forget that the integrity of the subject is founded on this inquisitive attention and on the gift of a voice can have dire consequences. The voice in itself is a means of revelation for the Jewish people. Forgetting this immemorial element, a dark element, a flaw in the depiction of an immortal, eternal subject, all-powerful, present, full of light, etc., opens the way to tyranny by a thing, an idea, a grandiose project such as the conquest of an empire, its rule and expansion.

> A nothing
> we were, we are, we will
> remain, flowering:
> the Nothing—, the
> NoOnesRose.[23]

In the Almond—what stands in the almond?
Nothingness.
What stands in the Almond is Nothingness.
There it stands and stands.

 In Nothingness—what stands there? The King.
There the King stands, the King.
There he stands and stands.[24]

Forgetting the unthinkable anguish, forgetting the primal repression which re-presses Nothing although nothing is repressed, no representation, but the void is an-nulled. Forgetting primal repression means forgetting that Nothing is not repressed, that the void is counterinvested. The abyss (*Abgrund*, literally the "bottomless") is counterinvested. This counterinvestment closes the road to the abyss. This obstacle provides a foundation for the subject, for memory and temporality, out of almost nothing: the attention of a friendly voice—the prayer of the soul, Celan says, quoting Walter Benjamin who was quoting Malbranche. This is the revelation, the message carried by the stigmatised people, which opposes the discourse of the "it", of the neutral, reminding us that humanity stands on the imperfect and the fragile that sutures the void by means of the encounter between an I and a Thou.

The poem stands fast at the edge of itself; it calls and brings itself [...] back from its "already-no-longer" into its "always-still". [In the drafts:] In this in-between, the space of its becoming free, in statu nascendi thus and [...] also in statu moriendi, this, its own groundlessness, the poem takes as its ground. But he who walks on his head, has the sky below him as an abyss.[25]

Here, Celan is alluding to another of Büchner's protagonists, Lenz, to whom the poet referred in his Darmstadt speech in September 1960. Lenz is the one who was sometimes annoyed that he could not walk on his head.

He who walks on his head, ladies and gentlemen [...], has the sky beneath him-self as an abyss. [...] Lenz—or rather Büchner—has here gone a step further than Lucile. His "Long live the King" is no longer a word, it is a terrifying fall-ing silent, it takes away his—and our—breath and words.[26]

I am frozen into silence when those around me, the one on whom I depend to ex-ist as a subject, to keep standing (*stehen* is one of the most frequently used words in Celan's poetry), turns away and falls silent. If in this environment there is only neu-tral discourse, a discourse which negates the shadow, forgets originary terror, the bottomlessness on which everything stands, itself included, then I gasp for breath.
Celan's poetry depicts this breathlessness. It does so through the use of rhetori-cal devices such as broken words, dislocated like someone's limbs might be; or

monosyllabic verses like the cries heard in the torture chamber where screams are voiced in all languages.

> *Wann*
> *wannblühen, wann,*
> *wannblühen die, hühendiblüh,*
> *huhendiblu, jasie, die September-*
> *rosen?*

> When,
> when do they bloom, when
> will they bloom, the, hühendibloom,
> hudediblue, yes them, the September-
> roses?

> Hüh—*on tue*... Yes, when?
> When, when when,
> Delusion when, yes, delusion, —
> Brother
> Blinded, brother
>   Extinguished, you read,
> you read and you,
> this here, this:
> Dis-
> parateness—: When
> will it bloom, the When,
> the Wherefrom, the Whereto and What,
> and who
> lives out of—and to—and toward—
>   oneself, the axis—
> tone, Tellus, in its soul—
> [...]
> The tone, oh,
> the Oh-tone, ah,
> the A and the O
> the Oh–these–gallows–already–again, the Ah–it–thrives.[27]

Another device is a mix of languages, like in the torture chamber. The "*on tue*" springs up suddenly between two German syllables. Celan also knows how to play with languages to hide-show, as he does with the word "people" and the phrase "concede no word to what happened":

> I saw my poplar go down to the water,
> *[Ich sahmeinePappelhinabgehnzum Wasser]*
> I saw its arm reach down into the depth,
> I saw its roots beg skyward for night.[28]

Pappel is assonant with the French word "peuplier" (which comes from *popu-lus*), and resembles the word "people". Recourse to this word allows Celan to avoid the terrible German word, saturated with terror, *das Volk*.

We write ourselves […], with the poem therefore, the poem remaining most pain-fully mindful of all the experiences and shocks we write ourselves toward a neces-sary, inalienable reality—: in word-shape—whatelse could it be?—, open on all sides, we venture, and that is at times unpleasant, into the word—and answerless.[29]

This is when you take the road into yourself, to your ownmost suffering, that you stand with your voiceless thought, your breath suspended, in the pause that reminds you of your heart, and you don't speak of it. And later, only later, you speak of you. It is in the space of this "later" that I insert my digging in the crevasse of time, where I dig and dig tirelessly.

> THERE WAS EARTH INSIDE THEM, and they dug.
> They dug and dug [but, being
> > made of earth, they dig into
> > themselves]. […]
> > O you dig and I dig, and I dig myself
> > > toward you,
> > and on our finger the ring awakens.[30]

I dig a passage to you and only when I reach you can I experience what happened and find the words—later—that set me free, and set you free. Analysis as writing is in this movement, in this process of digging in which I will be able to recognise your breath when you are almost covered over, and separate it from the voices in you which discourage you, forbid you to become distinct, to separate, whisper that you should stay silent, don't make a fuss, because "everyone has troubles and time heals all wounds".

Analysis is having the courage to stay the course, to stay focused on this Other, on the *infans* whose rhythm was thwarted. The analysand and the analyst are "on the alert", as Celan says. And no one can say how much longer the pause that sus-pends the breath, governs thinking and induces vigilance will last. The Captain in Büchner's play *Woyzeck* laments: "There's a real wind out there, I can feel it. Makes my back prickle, as if a mouse w's running up and down it". And Celan asks:

> "Enlarge art?"
> No. On the contrary, take art with you into your innermost narrowness. And set yourself free.[31]

Enlarge psychoanalysis? No. Take analysis with you into your innermost nar-rowness. And set yourself free. The work of analysis? Imitating Celan when he speaks of the poem, I will use his words to conclude:

> Craft means handiwork, a matter of hands. And these hands must belong to *one* person, i.e. a unique, mortal soul searching for its way with its voice and its dumbness. Only truthful hands write true poems. I cannot see any basic differ-ence between a handshake and a poem.[32]

Notes

1   Celan, P., *"Was geschah?"* in *Memory Rose into Threshold Speech*, p. 325.
2   Lyotard, J.-F., *Heidegger and "the Jews"*, Minneapolis, MN, University of Minnesota Press, 1990.
3   Levi, P., *The Drowned and the Saved*, New York, Simon & Schuster, 2017, pp. 83–84.
4   Celan, P., "Singbarer remnant" in *Breathturn into Timestead*, New York, Farrar, Straus and Giroux, 2022.
5   Celan, P., "Stretto" in *Memory Rose into Threshold Speech*, Joris, P. (Trans.), New York, Farrar, Straus and Giroux, 2020.
6   Celan, P., "Edgar Jené and the Dream about the Dream", *Collected Prose*, London, Psychology Press, 2003.
7   Celan, P., "Death Fugue" in *Memory Rose into Threshold Speech*, op. cit.
8   Celan, P., *The Meridian: Final Version — Drafts — Materials*, Joris, P. (Trans.), Redwood City, CA, Stanford University Press, 2011.
9   *Ibid.*, p. 128.
10 Améry, J., *At the Mind's Limits*, Bloomington, IN, Indiana University Press, 1980.
11 Celan, P., *Breathturn into Timestead*, op. cit. p.19.
12 Celan, P., "Speak, You Too" in *The Meridian: Final Version — Drafts — Materials*, op. cit.
13 Büchner, G., *Danton's Death*, London, Methuen, 1983.
14 Celan, P., *The Meridian: Final Version — Drafts — Materials*, op. cit.
15 *Ibid.*
16 Celan, P., *Correspondance (1951–1970)*, Paris, Seuil, 2001.
17 Kafka, F., *Letters to Friends, Family and Editors*, New York, Schocken Books, 1977.
18 Celan, P., *The Meridian: Final Version — Drafts — Materials*, op. cit.
19 *Ibid.*, p. 127.
20 Celan, P., "In the Air" in *Memory Rose into Threshold Speech*, op. cit., p. 358.
21 Celan, P., *"Lob der Ferne"* (Praise of Distance) in *Selected Poems and Prose*, New York, W.W. Norton, 2002.
22 Celan, P., "Everything Is Different", in *Memory Rose into Threshold Speech*, op. cit., p. 347.
23 Celan, P., "Psalm" in *Memory Rose into Threshold Speech*, op. cit.
24 Celan, P., "Mandorla" in *Memory Rose into Threshold Speech*, op. cit.
25 Celan, P., *The Meridian: Final Version — Drafts — Materials*, op. cit., p. 8 and p. 60.
26 *Ibid.* p. 7.
27 Here, I hear Celan say, among other things: "The one who does not hear *Wannsee* in *Wannwann* drives me crazy". Celan, P., "Huhediblu", in Memory Rose into Threshold Speech, op. cit., p. 332.
28 Celan, P., "I Heard It Said", in *Memory Rose into Threshold Speech*, op. cit., p. 87.
29 *Ibid.*, p. 66.
30 Celan, P., "There Was Earth Inside Them", in *Memory Rose into Threshold Speech*, op. cit., p. 245.
31 Celan, P., *The Meridian: Final Version — Drafts — Materials*, op. cit. p.10.
32 Celan, P., "Letter to Hans Bender", in *Collected Prose*, Oxford, Routledge, 2003, p. 26.

11

Bearing the Other
The Two-Stage Birth of Psychoanalysis

Rather than recounting the birth of a psychoanalyst, that is, my coming into being as an analyst, I will write a parable conveying the birth of psychoanalysis: its
invention by Freud in 1900 and its revelation by Ferenczi in 1930. This parable
does not pretend to present the exact truth about what analysis was for Freud or
for Ferenczi, but I will use this story—my way of understanding it—to tell, in a
roundabout fashion, the story of my own "birth" as an analyst.

Psychoanalysis was not born in 1900, with the publication of *The Interpretation
of Dreams*, but in 1930, when Ferenczi brought into question the position held by
his analyst, his master and friend, when he opposed Freud, reminding him of the
founding principle of psychoanalysis, which Freud himself had stated in 1892—
while collaborating with Breuer—a principle affirming that hysterics suffer from
reminiscences.

In a letter dated January 11, 1930, Freud tells Ferenczi that he has noticed signs
of alienation on the part of the latter. He points out that his friend does not mention
the invitation to come to Vienna, speaks strangely of the impression made on him
by the "Professor's book" (*Civilisation and Its Discontents*), [1] ignored "some jocu-
lar and tender things" in earlier letters, and has adopted a new "objectivity"[2] in
his relations with Freud. Ferenczi agrees and takes this opportunity to say that his
hostility is directed towards the analyst Freud was for him:

> I was especially sorry that you did not comprehend and bring to abreaction
> in the analysis the partly only transferred negative feelings and fantasies [the
> hatred and anger, no doubt, voiced in the Oxford lecture].[3]

Freud answered that at the time they did not yet realise that these reactions could
be expected in all cases. He asks Ferenczi ironically: "how long this analysis would
have had to last until the inimical impulses in our excellent relationship had succeeded in getting through".

Freud suggests to Ferenczi that his unresolved "brother complex" had been reac-
tivated.[4] Indeed, Freud, who cannot conceive that he might have nurtured negative
feelings and fantasies towards his analysand, displays an attitude of denial, as so
many parents do. But when he blames Ferenczi's "brother complex", he goes even

DOI: 10.4324/9781003435730-13

further. Indeed, by doing this Freud sets in place a "scientific" prohibition to his analysand's attempt to explore the analyst's psychic spheres. He excludes the possibility of the analyst's transference to the analysand.

When the analysand—in this case Ferenczi—is asked to see in his unconscious productions (dreams, slips of the tongue, effects of transference) the influence of a complex (fraternal or paternal), he is diverted from a detour, from a mediation. And this deviation is the equivalent of repeating the childhood trauma, because it leads the subject astray (*seducere*, in Latin), turning him away from the complexity of the determinants at work in the particular course of his life. Here, Ferenczi discovers Freud's original inclination, and with it seduction theory and deflection. In this case, Ferenczi, like Dora 30 years earlier, was asked to act "as if" his analyst was not subjectively involved in the relationship established between them, in the transference.

An explanation[5]—called Oedipian—is necessarily true. Its truth is unyielding, like an authoritative argument, always clever enough to mask, to repress, the intersubjective context, that is, that which emanates from the analyst. When Freud refers Ferenczi to his "brother complex", he becomes a seducer who suggests to the analysand that he stop his inquiry and turn his back at once on the complexity of his ties to the analyst, on the decisive elements coming from the latter, just as in his childhood he might have been induced to ignore such decisive elements coming from his parent. One paradoxical aspect of this situation is that Freud asks the analysand to end his inquiry in the name of Oedipus. Thus, Freud exhibits, on the one hand, the image of an Oedipus desirous of pursuing the inquiry to arrive at the truth at all costs, and on the other hand, the unscrupulous image of Jocasta, determined to stop the inquiry at once.

The violence with which Freud refuses to consider his own hatred, his own negative feelings, in his relationship with Ferenczi, would have significant consequences, to say the least, for the psychoanalytic movement. This position opened the way for the application of the theory to the practice, like a ready-made piece of clothing placed on a mannequin. This image represents the original ailment of the discipline, which was created as if amputated. It would be up to Ferenczi's followers, among whom we count Imre Hermann, Michael Balint, D.W. Winnicott, Harold Searles, Gisela Pankow, Nicolas Abraham and Maria Torok, to correct this amputation that I liken to the cutting away, the disavowal of soul murder, of a psychic catastrophe. Later, Winnicott would find this fragment of the Real, and would speak of psychic breakdown in his famous posthumous article that lacks only one thing: a reference to the first analyst who asserted the unthinkable existence of such a catastrophe—Ferenczi. The figure of the analyst as seducer—seducer because amputated—created the analyst Sphinx, *Homo psychanalyticus*, as François Perrier said, the analyst Ferenczi had described in his Oxford speech a few months earlier.

* * *

On March 8, 1932, Ferenczi confided to his *Diary* the discouragement he felt at hearing himself "constantly accused of being an assassin" by a patient. He even recollects the "tragic" moment in his own childhood when his mother accused him of making her "die of sorrow".

> This [accusation of murder] was the occasion for me to plunge into […] my own infantile experiences: the tragic childhood moment when the mother declares: you are killing me.[6]

Ferenczi had just understood that in his practice he reproduces the attitude he adopted when he desperately wanted to avoid the accusation that he made his mother suffer. This accusation is diabolical because the child, unless he is supported by a third person, for instance the father, is unable to take stock of the kind of trap in which he is held. In metaphysical terms, he is unable to translate the displeasure focused on him, that is, to turn around in order to feel such a sensation again, reflect on it and possibly locate its source, in himself as well as in his parent. To convert displeasure into a sensation and connect it with the fact that he bears the other—and finally be able to say: "I cannot bear him"—the child needs a witness. But, unfortunately, often the child is not aware of any displeasure, so that this nameless unpleasantness is an annoyance that insists but has no existence. Hence, the child cannot recognise it and, unable to turn against it, he has no choice but to bear the "suffering" the parent does not know he bears.

At a decisive moment, Ferenczi became aware that he impelled his analysand—in the sense of "appealing" to her—to play the role of his own mother when he acted as therapist with her—a truly prodigious therapist. Ferenczi had placed himself in the position of one who ensures the existence of a wounded parent, instead of the reverse situation, and he had felt the pain associated with a catastrophe unknown to his mother, while sacrificing his own inner space and time.

This figure of the prodigious therapist is what Ferenczi has been questioning for several years, officially since August 1929 when, at the Eleventh Congress of the International Psychoanalytical Association held in Oxford, he gave his address entitled "Relaxation Principle and Neo-Catharsis".[7] In this paper, Ferenczi opposes "a rigid and cold aloofness on the analyst's part [which can only produce] infantile opposition to adult authority". He has discovered that his patients "did not dare to rebel openly against [a] didactic and pedantic attitude of the analyst". He suggests that analysts adopt a more humble attitude and, if necessary, admit the errors they might have made.[8]

But Ferenczi, who has turned back on himself, has rebelled against himself in light of the analysis conducted with this patient, does not consider the matter closed; he does not leave Freud to his obstinate resistance, and renews his attempts to convince him. I bet he knew his analyst well enough to know that love of truth and the courage he has already displayed in the past would one day bring him out of his refusal to concede. A few months after the 1930 exchange of letters, Ferenczi opposes Freud again in Vienna, where he reads to his ailing master a paper to be presented at the Psychoanalytic Congress in Wiesbaden, entitled "Confusion of the Tongues Between the Adult and the Child". Ferenczi is suggesting to his master who has been repeating for three years that he is on the wrong track, that in fact psychoanalytic technique has regressed since the "traumatic element" was neglected, and that this has led to hasty explanations invoking the Oepidus complex in every situation, and even to the use of notions like "disposition" and "constitution". When analysts base their practice on these premises, Ferenczi writes, their results are fleeting because they have ignored the feelings of hate and anger accumulated between them and their patients. Patients can still have these feelings of "hatred and rage" when the analyst refuses to acknowledge that "the patients have an exceedingly refined sensitivity for the tendencies [...] of their analyst, even if the analyst is completely unaware of this sensitivity".[9] And he adds:

> Here, however, we meet with considerable resistances, this time [...] in ourselves as well as in our patients. [...] A great part of the repressed criticism felt by our patients is directed towards what might be called *professional hypocrisy*.[10]

The hypocrisy referred to here protects the analyst from realising that he has turned the analysand into his therapist, that is, someone willing to bear with him for fear that he may break down. This situation reproduces the one occurring in childhood when a "wise baby"—as Ferenczi recognises himself to have been—or a "prodigious therapist" is able to safeguard his parent's existence, that is, to preserve order in the universe, the ground under his feet and the sky above his head. All other considerations aside, in his analysis with Freud, Ferenczi had not been able to abandon the position of model student, another attribute of the prodigious therapist, a place many children are used to holding. In Wiesbaden, like in Oxford, Ferenczi says: "With this cold reserve, the childhood situation is repeated [...] and it is no wonder that this attitude produces the same results as the initial trauma". Instead of contradicting such an important person, his patients had preferred to identify with him.[11]

Following this presentation in Wiesbaden, Ferenczi had to face an armed guard who suddenly sprung up in Freud to prevent the child "still alive" in him to gain access to his own catastrophe. And this guard, who appeared instantly given the danger of rebellion, was supported at once by the inner circle of Freud's disciples: Max Eitingon, Abraham Brill, Johan Van Ophuijsen and above all Ernst Jones. They all found the presentation "scandalous" and were determined to forbid its publication. These disciples, with Jones in the lead, would soon slander Ferenczi and spread the notion that he has lost his mind.

* * *

When Ferenczi recognised and translated the message he unknowingly incited his analysand to address to him, he accomplished a turning-around. When he became aware that he had prompted his patient to respond to a demand he did not know he had made, when he realised and acknowledged that the patient–analyst transference had been inverted, he revealed psychoanalysis to itself and set the ground for relegating the notion of countertransference—so heavily ideologically burdened—to epistemological history. At the same time, he was leaving behind the notion of the analyst's "error", which he had still used at the Oxford Congress. The error and guilt of the analyst now became signs that the latter had become the locus of suffering.

When Ferenczi opposed his analyst, he created an opening in the system of defense mechanisms where Freud had stored unconsciously—but not in accordance with the unconscious as he theorised it—a familiar being who had suffered a breakdown. Freud had not been able to explore this system because, to do this, he first had to prompt a Ferenczi, an analyst–analysand who could identify and name what Freud had stored inside himself but could not own, since it had not been passed down to him.

Freud, the creator of psychoanalysis, had adopted Goethe's adage: "What you inherit from your father must first be earned before it's yours", but he could not earn what had not been marked with the negative sign that enables the attribution of a word to designate a sensation, a "thing". For the subject to be able to inherit a *thing*, this thing must exist independently of him, in his absence—it must bear the mark of the negative. This is what Freud teaches in the essay "Negation", when he states that negation is the *successor*, the heir, of the drive towards destruction, while assertion is a phenomenon belonging to the Eros, the unifying instinct.[12] Ferenczi's presentation pointed to what had been transmitted to Freud but not inherited by him, that which he had swallowed but which had no existence because it was unnamable.

The theory of repression, resolutely on the side of speech, translation and dreamwork, had been the precondition of the expulsion of the "vulture". Another precondition had been the presence next to Freud of a Ferenczi likely to have the courage to contradict the "paternal hypothesis", and to remind the one claiming the position of father of the discipline, of the foundations of that discipline.

Ferenczi gave up the position of model student, gave up being the figure of Freud's secret prodigious therapist. By doing this, he opened a new research perspective of which we benefit to the present day in a practice that takes into account the fact that although the analyst and the analysand are in an asymmetrical relationship, they are in the same situation in the transference. By forsaking his role as therapist, Ferenczi symbolically forced Freud to get back to work, to bring into question the figure of the prodigious therapist, of the sentry, the unattainable guide, which emerges when the turn-around takes place. And it is with Ferenczi—after his death—that Freud writes some of his last texts, like *A Disturbance of Memory on the Acropolis*, *Splitting of the Ego in the Process of Defence*, and above all *Moses and Monotheism*. Before he died, Ferenczi invited his master and friend to draw all the appropriate conclusions from his own discovery; he revealed psychoanalysis to itself.

Notes

1 Freud, S., *Civilisation and Its Discontents*, S.E. 21, London: Hogarth.
2 Freud, S., and Ferenczi, S., "Letter January 11, 1930", in *The Correspondence of Sigmund Freud and Sandor Ferenczi*, Vol. 3, Cambridge, MA, The Belknap Press of Harvard University Press, 2000, p. 380.
3 Or, depending on how this illegible word is decyphered—*mir* or *nur*—"in part transferred by me". Freud, S., and Ferenczi, S., "Letter January 17, 1930", *Ibid.*, p. 382.
4 Freud, S., and Ferenczi, S., "Letter January 20, 1930", *Ibid.*, p. 386.
5 Here, "explanation" seems more appropriate than "interpretation".
6 Ferenczi, S., *The Clinical Diary of Sandor Ferenczi*, Cambridge, MA, Harvard University Press, 1995.
7 Ferenczi, S., "The Principle of Relaxation and Neocatharsis". *The International Journal of Psychoanalysis*, 11, 1930, 428–443.
8 The use of the word "error" shows that Ferenczi still had a way to go to understand the full impact of the intersubjectivity at work in analysis, as Searles would teach us later.
9 When Ferenczi adds that this anger is often due to the fact that "patients gradually become better analysed than we […] are" he is no doubt referring to the particular situation in which he was in analysis with Freud, the original unanalysed psychoanalyst, the first analyst who had not experienced what the analysand was experiencing. I am tempted to see this not as a universal, but as a frequent occurrence. In my case, before I underwent the analytic experience to which I have alluded here obliquely, I felt that my patients were benefitting from a better analysis than mine had been.
10 Ferenczi, S., "Confusion of the Tongues Between the Adult and the Child", *The International Journal of Psycho-Analysis*, 30: 225–230, 1949.
11 As Ferenczi pointed out, many analysands who feel they must safeguard their analyst's existence identify with him, and by doing this become analysts. They in fact swallow the analyst to spare him hardship, to avoid the risk of seeing him break down.
12 Freud, S. (1925), *Negation,* S.E. 19, London: Hogarth.

Contribution to a Discussion on Bion's Work

A comment made by Bion about the Oedipus complex gives me the opportunity to reopen the discussion on the universality of this complex.

> If we now turn to the question of what makes reality so hateful in the eyes of the patient that he is *forced* to kill the Ego which brings him in contact with it, it seems natural to suppose that it is the sexual aspect of the Oedipal situation.[1]

In my opinion, Bion is not formulating his thoughts adequately in this passage. In truth, it's the refusal of the environment to accept aggressivity, agonising terror, that destroys the Ego. The refusal, the impossibility of accepting the kind of pain that agonising terror can produce amounts to the refusal of instinct altogether. Why? Because, as Winnicott did, I believe that near the origin drive is unified and the *destrudo* is only one of its aspects.

Indeed, Freud had mentioned a unified drive briefly in 1919, when he put forth the hypothesis of a life-and-death instinct. I say "mentioned" because a few lines later he abandoned this hypothesis, without erasing it, and went back to dual drive theory. He justified this decision by invoking common sense. I have discussed elsewhere that psychoanalytic research after Freud has consisted of questioning this appeal to common sense, and the terror that dual drive causes in the theoretical domain.

Making room for good sense is what Bion was doing when he spoke of an "innate Oedipal preconception". I suggest that we consider this preconception to be nothing other than the paradoxical potential which defines the child, and that this potential defines the Oedipus complex. I believe that psychoanalysis was accepted as a new field of knowledge and a new practice because Freud discovered the Oedipus complex. Moreover, the field remains alive when analysts base their practice on its particularity, that is, the paradoxical nucleus that Freud discovered not in 1900, but in 1923, as he pursued his research. Such a nucleus is called an entelechy in Aristotelian language, the entelechy of the Oedipus complex, in the same way as "axety" would be an attribute of the axe. Soul, power, entelechy, wellspring, principle... these are all terms that could designate this nucleus. And this nucleus, this principle, is condensed in the paradoxical injunction Freud states in *The Ego*

DOI: 10.4324/9781003435730-14

and the Id: "You ought to be like this (like your father", along with the prohibition: "You may not be like this (like your father)".[2]

This injunction, which Freud described a few lines earlier as being the "broad general outcome of the sexual phase dominated by the Oedipus complex", contradicts the psychologising discourses about Oedipus, a theme used and overused by Freud himself and some of his overly loyal disciples, to the point of harming analysands who had suffered psycho-corporal trauma. Freud and these analysts were acting as if their patients were able to sustain a paradox. They thought the problem had been solved and were trying to "Oedipise" their patients on the Procustrean bed where they had them recline.

I maintain that the specificity of the Oedipus complex, its essence, that which makes it a foundation, is this paradoxical injunction submitted to the subject. But for the *infans* to be able to obey such an injunction, he must have had time to acquire a paradoxical foundation by experiencing a period in which he and his mother are one, in which the baby becomes the breast (or the mother), in which the object is the subject. The *infans* must have had the experience of taking forcefully the object placed before him; of creating the breast offered him. The same applies to all other functions. The gift of a paradoxical foundation is the gift a mother makes when, with the baby, she accepts the union of contradictory feelings like love and hate, seduction and restraint, alternating rhythmic continuity–discontinuity, infinite assent and punctual negation.

In a different situation, when the *infans* has not been given such a paradoxical foundation, he finds himself captive to the One, to the same, and attempts pathetically to escape the harm that the union of contradictions inflicts on him. He attempts to escape by throwing himself frantically into an endless dance of *all or nothing*. For the analysand who tries to play his role, the Oedipus is unknown territory, as Bion said, and the triad is a problem for him. But what is the triad? Not much, almost nothing, only the connection that brings together two contradictory injunctions: "You ought to be like your father" *and* "You may not be like your father". This paradox specific to the Oedipus complex does, *in fact, pose a problem* for the analysand who, as a baby, did not receive the gift of such a potentiality. This figure, which links the same with the other, disturbs the one who has been accustomed to deal with the same, to avoid the whole in order to fall back on nothing, and to plunge into the all to escape the nothing; or else to play tricks with the same to change it into other, even if he has to kill it or kill himself. This is how I understand Bion's suggestion when he says: "In these cases the distinction is not between conscious and unconscious, but between finite and infinite"[3]—where I interpret "infinite" to be the infernal dance of the same, that is, the dance of *all or nothing*.

An analyst I know answered the question of whether or not analysis is Oedipian in the negative, adding that "Oedipus" has become the name of the normative notion, the most misleading there is; that the normative confuses the solution with the problem; and that the psycho-corporal is not entirely Oedipian and includes elements unrelated to the Oedipus. I agree with all this, but would formulate it somewhat differently. I would say that, on the contrary, psychoanalysis is entirely

Oedipian, provided we do not psychologise the Oedipus complex, as Freud did for a long time; provided we extract from the mine he opened the active element, his principle, his entelechy, that is, the paradoxical injunction: "You ought to be like your father *and* you may not be like your father".

Furthermore, although the colleague I mentioned says that in the case of the Wolf ManFreud shows that repression and foreclosure coexist, I take this to be not a reality, but the sign of remnants of a "dream" of Freud's embedded in the foundation of psychoanalysis. "What dream?", you might ask. The desire that it be possible to establish a course of uninterrupted meaning, as is the case with Oedipus-centered psychology, to which Freud remained loyal until he discovered the reality of splitting in the last year of his life.

The existence of a discontinuity of being, caused by an inadequate environment, requires the analyst to adopt a humble and rigorous attitude, contrary to the attitude Freud displayed with Fliess and with his patients. This is so because in these cases the analyst is asked to expose himself to storms, to acting out, to the frenzy of *all or nothing*; during these sudden storms, he must show unlimited patience, bear the blows and survive, because he becomes—as psychotic transference would have it—cold, insensitive, narrow-minded, arrogant or stupid. Here, the analyst becomes a stand-in for the antagonistic object that was curious about the *infans* but could not bear to be the container of nameless emotions, like those provoked by the fear of dying. Bion summarised an essential aspect of his teaching when he wrote that the maternal function consists of transforming, of "symbolising", unnamed pains and emotions.

> From the infant's point of view she [the mother] should have taken into her, and thus experienced, the fear that the child was dying. [...] [She] could not tolerate experiencing such feelings and reacted [...] by denying them ingress...[4]

When Freud asserted the coexistence of repression and foreclosure in his essay on the Wolf Man[5]—a coexistence he described as the solution adopted by the fetishist—the answer he was providing resembled the answer Oedipus gave the Sphinx. His arrogance was as great as that of Oedipus—another name for Freud, as our colleague remarked quite rightly. When an analyst gives an Oedipian psychological explanation to an analysand filled with a nameless emotion, the Ego of the latter is violently attacked. The Ego of the *infans* instantly disappears from the analytic scene. Sometimes the patient leaves the analyst, or he swallows him, as Oedipus swallowed the Sphinx. In that case, there is no analysand left, there is only a two-headed monster, an analyst–analysand or an analysand–analyst, turned ventriloquist. The conflict brought by the analysand has been extinguished by incorporation. The analysis is over, or it becomes interminable.

Freud's solution in the case of the Wolf Man was not the right one because the coexistence of repression and foreclosure is an illusion that can only last for short periods of time. In moments of crisis, repression bursts into bits, it is swept away. On this, I completely agree with Bion. We might say that the coexistence of mechanisms of repression and foreclosure is a false coexistence, a lure to hide the contour of a fracture, of the discontinuity of being. Neither Bion nor Winnicott believed in this coexistence, which led to the forced march of Oedipian campaigns, to "Oedipianisation". Bion rightly pointed out that dispersed fragments of the Oedipus do not constitute an Oedipus complex and do not lead to the resolution of this complex.

These reflections lead to re-examining the questions of debt and guilt, and asking whether they in fact originate in the question of the father. This has been the perspective from which they have been viewed, the only one possible as long as the founding paradox—the triad—was associated with the decline and resolution of the Oedipus complex. This being so, as soon as the founding paradox of human existence is brought close to the psycho-corporal origin, it becomes clear that the creation of a triad composed of two contrary elements indissociably connected depends on what Winnicott qualified rather vaguely as the "environment". The principle, the triad made up of two contrary elements linked by the conjunction "and", is inscribed in the mother, or not. If it is not, the father's efforts to be recognised in his paternal role will meet with considerable opposition.

* * *

Our research was sparked by the fact that Freud confused the repression of representations with the defense mechanisms displayed by Fliess. He and Freud had been each-other's *Nebenmensh* until the day when Fliess refused to admit having made a professional error. This refusal revealed to Freud the ethical catastrophe his friend embodied, and this revelation caused him to end the friendship. This event had repercussions for psychoanalysis because this separation swept away the figure of the *Nebenmensh*, just as a landslide would do with a house. After this event, Freud's theoretical work was resolutely directed towards the ontology of drives, and the psycho-corporal development of the *infans* became in great measure dependent on the innate intensity of drives, described as existing in opposed pairs such as self-preservation/sex drives, Ego drives/sex drives, and finally life instincts/death instincts. But this new orientation brought no fundamental change.

Within the logic of these drive theories which excluded the human environment entirely, notions of psychosexual development and transference became incongruous. As a result, the three principles forming the axiomatic corpus of Freud's theory, that is, the connection between body and psyche, transference, and the primacy of the sexual, were disconnected from each other. This incompatibility between the practice and the principles that held up the theory was the major symptom of the childhood illness of psychoanalysis. Freud's successors, after Ferenczi—who was the first disciple to be disloyal through a sense of loyalty—had to restore the initial conditions of transference, starting with the source of *the* drive.

The path I travelled was opened by Ferenczi when he turned around to oppose Freud, risking the overturning of the psychoanalytical edifice. Ferenczi reinstated the notion of seduction, and introduced the crucial notion of introjection, which reiterated what Freud had designated as "external influences". But this time these influences were attributed to the mother–baby relation, to the "dual unity", to use Nicolas Abraham's apt expression. Ferenczi says:

> I described introjection as a mechanism allowing the extension to the external world of self-erotic interest in the origin, by the introduction of outer objects into the sphere of the ego.[6]

By doing this, Ferenczi connected drive with transference, economy with dynamics. This point of reversal heralded an upheaval in psychoanalytic theory. Later, Winnicott expressed the same idea more figuratively, saying: "There is no such thing as a baby".[7]

Thanks to the notions of dual unity and introjection, the source of the drive could now take is rightful place in the definition of a fundamental concept. "We then see how greatly the simple pattern of the physiological reflex is complicated by the introduction of instincts".[8] Once the source of the instinct is traced back to the dual unity, to the initial conditions the *infans* encounters in his environment, metapsychology, transference, sexuality (and aggression) become compatible, and the drive is unified. This instinctual monism was to relegate dualism and death drive to the history of concept development.

Notes

1 Bion, W.R., "On Arrogance" in *Second Thoughts*, London, William Heineman Medical Books, 1967.
2 Freud, S., *The Ego and the Id*, S.E. 19, London: Hogarth.
3 Levy, F., "Bion avec Oedipe", Les Lettres de la SPF, no. 35, in *L'Oedipe de la psychanalyse, mythe ou complexe?* Paris, Campagne Première, 2016.
4 Bion, W.R., "Attacks on Linking", *International Journal of Psychoanalysis*, 40 (5–6), 1959.
5 Freud, S., *From the History of an Infantile Neurosis*, S.E. 17, London: Hogarth.
6 Ferenczi, S., *First Contributions to Psycho-Analysis*, Oxford, Routledge, 1952.
7 Winnicott, D.W., *The Child, the Family and the Outside World*, London, Penguin Books, 1991, p. 88.
8 Freud, S., *Instincts and Their Vicissitudes*, S.E. 14, London: Hogarth.

Index

For Product Safety Concerns and Information please contact our EU
representative GPSR@taylorandfrancis.com
Taylor & Francis Verlag GmbH, Kaufingerstraße 24, 80331 München, Germany